THE TRUTH IN OUR STORIES

THE TRUTH IN OUR STORIES

IMMIGRANT VOICES IN RADICAL TIMES

Edited by Mónica Tornoe, Elizabeth Wright,
and Jesús Jesse Esparza

IZZARD INK PUBLISHING
PO Box 522251
Salt Lake City, Utah 84152
www.izzardink.com

Copyright © 2022 by Mónica Tornoe / Undocumented Stories

All rights reserved. Except as permitted under the U.S. Copyright Act of 1976, no part of this publication may be reproduced, distributed, or transmitted in any form or by any means, or stored in a database or retrieval system, electronically or otherwise, or by use of a technology or retrieval system now known or to be invented, without the prior written permission of the author and publisher.

Library of Congress Cataloging-in-Publication Data
Names: Tornoe, Mónica, editor. | Wright, Elizabeth R. (Reverend), editor. |
   Esparza, Jesús Jesse, editor.
Title: The truth in our stories : immigrant voices in radical times /
   edited by Mónica Tornoe, Elizabeth Wright, and Jesús Jesse Esparza.
Other titles: Immigrant voices in radical times
Description: First edition. | Salt Lake City, Utah : Izzard Ink Publishing, [2022] |
   Includes bibliographical references.
Identifiers: LCCN 2022002892 (print) | LCCN 2022002893 (ebook) |
   ISBN 9781642280791 (paperback) | ISBN 9781642280807 (ebook)
Subjects: LCSH: Hispanic Americans—Biography. | Hispanic Americans—Social
   conditions. | Immigrants—United States—Social conditions.
Classification: LCC E184.S75 T79 2022 (print) | LCC E184.S75 (ebook) |
   DDC 305.868/073—dc23/eng/20220126
LC record available at https://lccn.loc.gov/2022002892
LC ebook record available at https://lccn.loc.gov/2022002893

Designed by Daniel Lagin
Cover Design by Andrea Ho
Photography by Joshua and Samuel Gandara

First Edition

Contact the author at info@izzardink.com

Paperback ISBN: 978-1-64228-079-1
eBook ISBN: 978-1-64228-080-7

Dedicated to all who hunger and thirst for justice . . . you shall be satisfied.

CONTENTS

Acknowledgments ix

Introduction xi

Part I
THE TRUTH IN *OUR STORIES*

1. Patricia Torres — 3
2. Jesús Salcido — 11
3. Sandra García — 19
4. Ángel Piedras — 27
5. Carmen Zuvieta — 35
6. Adrián Zamora — 45
7. Tony Ruiz — 55
8. Miriam Jaimes — 63
9. Elfega Torres — 71
10. María Elena Parra Martinez — 81
11. Raúl García — 91
12. Jean Carlo Vences — 99

Part II
THE TRUTH IN OUR STORIES

1. Immigrants Contribute	109
2. Immigrants Provide	111
3. Immigrants Deserve Dignity and Justice	113
Conclusion: The Challenge	119
Notes	125
Selected Bibliography	129

ACKNOWLEDGMENTS

With utmost sincerity, we wish to express our eternal gratitude to the brave women and men who contributed to this project as storytellers. This manuscript would not exist without their participation; thank you. We wish to acknowledge also the support from our respective institutions: Austin Presbyterian Theological Seminary; Justice for Our Neighbors, Austin Region; and Texas Southern University. We also wish to acknowledge that this project is supported by funding from the Institute for Diversity and Civic Life, made possible by a grant from the Henry Luce Foundation. To the team at Izzard Ink Publishing, we thank you for ensuring that all the necessary edits to the manuscript were done correctly and on time; the input was invaluable. To our amazing photographers, Joshua and Samuel Gandara from Cromatica, and to Mel Hummel, *mil gracias* for the work you all did. Special thanks to Melissa Wiginton for her support. Lastly, to all the individuals who allowed us to speak with them, and to the many others who contributed in different ways to the completion of this project, we thank you as well. Without your support, this project remains in its infancy.

INTRODUCTION

In an age of disinformation and growing racism, misconceptions about immigrants coupled with anti-immigrant sentiment have spread throughout American society. Consequently, the country has seen a concerning uptick in anti-immigrant rhetoric, harsh policies, and paramilitary activities; all of which threaten immigrant communities.

For more than a century, increases in immigration have been followed by a rise in nativism and resentment. After the war against Mexico in 1848, Mexican Americans found themselves in a rapidly changing world as the entire region west of the Mississippi River underwent a tremendous amount of transformation, resulting in their displacement, disenfranchisement, segregation, and exploitation.[1] While the Treaty of Guadalupe Hidalgo concluded the war between Mexico and the United States and established Mexican Americans as citizens of the US, the perception among those moving into the newly acquired territories was that they were foreigners who did not belong.

The turn of the twentieth century brought new industries such as the railroad, petroleum, and automobiles. Mexican immigrants, in search of work opportunities in these new trades, arrived in the US in record numbers, triggering a massive wave of nativism and anti-immigrant sentiment. The prevailing thought of the period among nativists was that immigrants were dirty, disease-carrying, dangerous foreigners with a predisposition for criminal behavior who competed against American-born workers for jobs. Additionally, they viewed immigrants, men particularly, as hypersexual, with lustful designs on white women. Certainly, they saw immigrants as biologically inferior, given their miscegenated racial make-up. Adding fuel to the fire was the fact that many immigrants spoke Spanish, and in a country where speaking a language other than English was unacceptable, this only exacerbated the entrenched anti-immigrant sentiment.

When the revolution broke out in Mexico in 1910, millions more immigrants, displaced by war, entered the US, sparking another wave of nativism. Many nativists believed immigrants to be radicals, espousing revolutionary sentiment toward the US government. Others labeled them anarchists and pointed to groups such as El Partido Liberal Mexicano, a revolutionary group that gained a foothold in the US in 1905 to support their positions against immigrants.[2] As the United States entered the First World War and thousands more immigrants arrived, immigrant bashing continued. With the war in full swing, those working for the agricultural firms either went off to fight or moved to urban centers to work in war-related industries, leaving the fields empty, and causing significant food shortages across the country.[3] However, coming to the rescue were the thousands of immigrants who filled that void by harvesting America's food. Subsequently, during the war immigrants fed Americans at home and American troops abroad. Yet their experiences in the US remained miserable. Compounding that misery was the Zimmerman Note, a 1917 telegram from Germany bound towards Mexico in which Germany asked Mexico to join it as an ally and invade the United States. Although Mexico refused the offer, once the note was made public it created massive anxiety, and immigrants found themselves again threatened, attacked, and criminalized. Federal authorities quickly surveilled immigrant communities while armed vigilante groups heavily patrolled them.[4]

During the 1920s, the nation saw the return of the Ku Klux Klan, the oldest domestic terrorist organization in the US. Part of its platform was a determination to expel all undesirables, including immigrants. Additionally, the nation saw the passage of the Immigration Act of 1924, which limited the number of people who could legally immigrate to the United States to 2 percent of each nationality's 1890 population each year. Known as quotas, this policy applied to all nations; however, the rate of allowable immigrant entrants was not equally applied. Countries with large Spanish-speaking, Catholic, Jewish, Islamic, and Asian populations had fewer application opportunities than their English-speaking, protestant counterparts. The Immigration Act of 1924 also officially created the US Border Patrol, the leading agency in militarizing the southern border.[5]

As the twenties pushed onward, nativists relied heavily on junk science to defend their opposition to immigrants and immigration. Known as the eugenics movement, its proponents argued that immigrants, Mexicans in particular, would negatively influence American society given their alleged biological inferiority. It further claimed that immigrants brought disease, crime, and poverty to the US by depressing wages and displacing American-born workers. Emerging from this racist science were several forms of punitive legislation targeting immigrants, including the Box Bill, a law introduced in 1926 that tried to bar immigration from all of Latin America. Nicknamed after John C. Box, a politician and bona fide eugenicist out of Texas, the legislation addressed the so-called Mexican Problem, that is, the problem of how to handle all the immigrants in the country. According to Box and other nativists, one solution was to remove immigrants from the country, but that was often too expensive and required massive labor. The easier fix was segregating them to the fields, as a separate labor force, thereby keeping them away from mainstream society.[6]

With the onset of the Great Depression, hostility against immigrants reached an all-time high as the federal government initiated an aggressive deportation campaign, the likes of which had never been seen before. Following the collapse of Wall Street, immigrants were blamed for the Depression, and then blamed again for prolonging it. Consequently, they became victims of a massive government-sanctioned deportation campaign that ultimately removed half a million people from the country, including many US-born Latinos. The campaign was swift, with raids often entering places of business. Tragically, countless families were broken up; those who resisted faced incarceration or worse. As could be expected, numerous vigilante groups formed and acted out their Depression-era frustrations on immigrant communities.[7] It was a terrifying experience.

During World War II, half a million Latinos served in the US Armed Forces, including more than fourteen thousand immigrants, such as Staff Sergeant Macario García, who served with the 4th Infantry Division and who received a Medal of Honor for acts of bravery in Europe.[8] Upon returning stateside, however, García was denied service in a restaurant in Texas due to Jim Crow policies like racial segregation and staunch anti-immigrant sentiment; García was a Mexican national at the time of his discharge from military service. Similar to World War I, there were again significant migration patterns. As agricultural workers left the fields for the front lines or the factories they created labor shortages, resulting in the governments of Mexico and the US instituting a guest worker program called the Bracero Program. This program brought workers from Mexico to the US to work in the agricultural industry and food-processing plants.[9] Strictly as a measure to deal with a wartime emergency, some two million men entered the US as temporary guest workers between 1942 and 1945. Just as during the First World War, these men harvested the foods that fed Americans at home and US troops abroad. Despite that service, however, their treatment while living and working in the country was nothing short of miserable, as braceros (immigrant workers) quickly became an exploitable labor force, earning starving wages, residing in unlivable accommodations, and falling prey to vicious attacks and other forms of harassment from ultra-nativists.[10]

This continued well into the next several decades, and gained momentum resulting from the Cold War. With the Second Red Scare (a series of witch trials perpetuated by the federal government against an alleged communist threat within the US) in full swing, Congress initiated a series of laws that adversely affected immigrant communities; the most notorious was something called Operation Wetback. This was a government-sponsored program designed to deport undocumented immigrants (Mexican and otherwise) from the US.[11] Despite the economic boom the US was experiencing following the Second World War, immigrants found themselves again accused of creating labor shortages and depressing wages. This old adage, coupled with new anxieties brought on by the Cold War, consequently resulted in a para-military campaign that ran over four years, beginning in 1954, and that deported countless people.[12] Similar to the raids that occurred during the Great Depression, numerous vigilante squads assisted government agents in these raids. The word *wetback* was a derogatory term used to identify unauthorized immigrants in the US, denoting how their backs got wet after swimming across the Rio Grande. This racial slur saturated every form of media in the country, helping it become the most common term used to vilify undocumented immigrants.[13]

Other laws passed in the postwar years that adversely affected immigrant communities included the Internal Security Act and the McCarran-Walter Act, which authorized the federal government to deport immigrants suspected of being in a communist organization, and which called for the denaturalization of immigrants accused of being communist sympathizers, respectively.[14] Punitive laws and aggressive action against immigrants continued into the sixties, with lesser success—admittedly due, of course, to the accomplishment of the Chicano Movement and its efforts to protect immigrant communities. In 1965, for example, activists were instrumental in convincing the federal government to legislate the Immigration Act of 1965, which opened the door for nonwhite immigrants to immigrate to the US, many of whom arrived as political refugees.[15] However, during the 1970s, the fight over immigrants' rights took center stage as the federal government moved swiftly to criminalize the undocumented.

Prompted by a massive stream of immigration from Latin America, the country in the 1970s would see another nativist resurgence, and the American people found themselves yet again in the middle of an intense fight. In the early 1970s, Mexico's economy was stagnating; jobs were scarce, and wages dropped. The economic situation there had grown bleak. As workers lost their jobs and their ability to sustain themselves and their families, many left for the US, hoping to find new employment opportunities, seeing no other alternative. However, as before, increased immigration into the country resurfaced a deep-rooted sense of anti-immigrant sentiment among the American population. Similar to previous decades, immigrants were depicted as criminals and portrayed as a threat. The US media again sensationalized this alleged threat, playing to American fears of foreign-born people. Responding to this alleged threat, the nativist politicians across several states introduced bills that punished immigrants and those who supported them. In 1971, for example, a bill known as the Dixon-Arnett Act was proposed, which promised to fine employers who hired undocumented workers.[16] A similar bill was presented the following year, taking it a step further by making it a felony to employ undocumented workers knowingly. In 1976, a bill that lowered the number of immigrants allowed to enter the US annually was proposed. Additionally, it proposed making parents of US-born children who had been deported, ineligible for applying for legal status. More heinous was the part of the bill that offered kids of undocumented parents' two options; accompany their deported parents or remain in the country and become wards of the courts.[17]

Also perpetuating the idea of an immigrant threat was the Immigration and Naturalization Services (INS), which initiated Operation Clean Sweep, another quasi-military-style campaign designed to deter what the INS considered an immigrant invasion. As part of this campaign, INS apprehended over half a million undocumented persons by 1973. Similar to raids from earlier decades, Operation Clean Sweep's net reached everywhere there was a sizable contingent of undocumented personnel. Like earlier campaigns, it too was saturated with allegations of abuse and other human rights violations.[18] As expected, mainstream media also helped frame the myth of an immigrant invasion, revving up the old argument that immigrants were criminals who took jobs away from "real" Americans. In 1977, for example, *Time Magazine* ran several articles propagating the myth that immigrant invaders were arriving in unprecedented numbers and costing the American taxpayer billions of dollars annually for their social services. Consequently, the myth of an immigrant invasion caused more hysteria among the American people, further alarming ultra-nativists and resulting in violent acts perpetrated against the undocumented, including but not limited to threats, harassment, coercion, extortion, wrongful arrests, kidnapping, physical attacks, sexual violence, and murder.[19]

In the 1980s, known as the Decade of the Hispanic, the fight over immigration again intensified as the number of immigrants increased exponentially. A collapse of Mexico's economy (the devaluation of the *peso* and the slashing of wages to mere cents on the dollar), coupled with several civil wars throughout Central America (El Salvador, Nicaragua, and Guatemala), uprooted millions of people, resettling them in the United States. It should also be noted that much of the military troubles in Central America resulted from direct clandestine involvement and interference by the United States. In El Salvador, for example, the US government financed the Salvadoran military to help it fend off attempts by a coalition of unionists, students, and activists who launched an armed struggle against the corrupt government of that nation. What followed was a bloody civil war that ultimately resulted in the deaths of 50,000 Salvadorans, primarily civilians. Consequently, hundreds of thousands fled to the US.[20]

In Nicaragua, President Ronald Reagan supported the counterrevolutionaries (Contras) against the Sandinista National Liberation Front (Sandinistas), the new revolutionary government in that nation. Fearing this new, leftist government would threaten US economic and political interests, the military, along with the CIA, backed operations against the new Nicaraguan government in what is called Reagan's "dirty little war." Here again, this conflict caused hundreds of thousands to flee to the US.[21] The same was true in Guatemala, where US forces financed and trained the Guatemalan military against revolutionary groups. As part of its strategy, the Guatemalan military deliberately attacked indigenous communities because they supported the revolutionary forces. In addition to burning their villages, the Guatemalan military incarcerated captives, subjecting them to extreme forms of torture and summary executions, leaving more than 200,000 people murdered. The result was a mass exodus of more than one million people from Guatemala, all of them bound for the US.[22]

As before, the large increase of immigrant refugees triggered a racist and nativist movement throughout the nation, particularly among those who took issue with what they considered the Latinization of the United States. To thwart this development, they initiated several bills that aimed to make it difficult for newcomers to navigate themselves in the country, such as California's Proposition 63, which made English the official language of that state. This bill and several others across the nation grew out of the English Only movement, which hoped to add an amendment to the US Constitution making English the "official" language of the country.[23] Proponents of this movement also lobbied for language in the Immigration Reform and Control Act of 1986 (the Amnesty bill), which promised to enforce sanctions on anyone who employed undocumented workers.[24] The rise in undocumented people also gave way to immigrant bashing. The bashing came from everywhere, including politicians who were pandering to their conservative and far-right anti-immigrant constituents and proposing bills that attempted to deny citizenship status to US-born children of undocumented immigrants.

During the 1990s, the federal government also spurred its efforts to complete and construct new border walls at several critical locations near the southern border. Additionally, the government effectively militarized the border with new agents and new weapons as part of the country's War on Drugs policy, which mistakenly equated America's drug problems with immigrants. The belief was that immigrants smuggled drugs into the US, getting the American people addicted.[25] Out of this policy came Operation Gatekeeper, a campaign to seal the border at critical ports of entry to prevent undocumented immigrants from crossing into the United States. Tragically, this policy has forced immigrants to find alternate and often far deadlier routes to the US, where they have fallen victims to dehydration, malnutrition, and death.[26]

As the nation entered the new millennium, anti-immigrant sentiment continued to embolden far-right groups, like the Minutemen, a paramilitary organization established in 2005 and composed of armed men who patrolled the southern border looking to detain immigrants. While they claimed to be "protecting" the country from immigrants, they did so without proper authorization, making them a hyperviolent vigilante group whose apprehensions of undocumented immigrants equated to kidnapping.[27]

One lesson to be learned from this brief history is that immigration has long been a controversial issue in American politics, affecting policies and people for over a century. It remains one of the most pressing issues in US history, dividing the nation along political, economic, moral, and ethical lines. Another lesson to be learned is that the narrative regarding immigration has long been distorted, depicting immigrants as dirty, disease-carrying criminals who corrupt our neighborhoods, depress our wages, overpopulate our prison systems, and drain our economy. This misshapen narrative, unfortunately, is not only historic but persists in our present time; therefore, we are publishing these stories to highlight the immigrant experience and hope to begin to change that perception. Their testimonies are unapologetically honest and reveal the horrid conditions that continue to characterize the lives of immigrants. We learn, for example, that immigrants cannot obtain a driver's license in most states and that they have unequal access to health care; they receive no benefits and work multiple jobs for unscrupulous employers who frequently exploit them.[28] Yet, there is hope because these stories help challenge the public narrative and dismantle the myths that engender their aggressive and clandestine persecution. Moreover, they provide a snapshot of the accomplishments of the immigrant community, revealing that immigrants improve the economy, are entrepreneurial, create jobs, pay taxes, and literally build the country's infrastructure. They also illustrate the untiring pursuits of a people typically believed to be apathetic about socioeconomic uplift and considered, unfortunately, unworthy of the American dream.

The hope is that this volume helps identify our misguided ways of thinking about the immigrant experience so that we can begin to eliminate the systemic racism on which our immigration system was built. By extension, we aim to transform a broken immigration system rooted in patriarchy and white supremacy. Additionally, we strive to challenge the existing and often inaccurate frameworks regarding the most criminalized and scapegoated community within the United States and beyond. The expectation is that this book will restore a sense of shared humanity with immigrants and the immigrant community.

THE TRUTH IN OUR STORIES

"The propagandist's purpose is to make one set of people forget that certain other sets of people are human."

—ALDOUS HUXLEY

PART I

The Truth in *Our Stories*

PATRICIA TORRES

"Nothing is more heartbreaking than to live with the crippling fear of losing a parent to deportation and having your family ripped apart."

—PATRICIA TORRES

I am the voice of many immigrants who are struggling to survive in this country. When Donald Trump was elected president, I remember the day my kids came home terrified because students were harassing them, saying, "Your mother is going to be deported." I tried not to cry in front of my children and to assure them that I would be safe. They were so worried because they had already experienced past emotional trauma. I told them: "We trust in God, right? So don't be scared." They were spending so much of their young lives filled with fear and anxiety, constantly worrying that their mama would be snatched away.

I was born the thirteenth child to two Mexican parents. Before I turned one, my mother fled Mexico for the United States, starting off in California, where my older siblings were already living. She came to the US to leave poverty and my abusive father.

Life was a different kind of hard in California. My family all worked in agriculture. I remember there was a series of immigration raids across the city. Sometimes they deported my older siblings. My entire family was devastated and unstable until the Immigration Reform and Control Act was signed into law by President Ronald Reagan on November 6, 1986, which legalized around three million immigrants, including my older siblings. This was such a relief for the entire family.

I like this quote from Ronald Reagan: "The problem of illegal immigration should not, therefore, be seen as a problem between the United States and its neighbors. Our objective is only to establish a reasonable, fair, orderly, and secure system of immigration into this country and not to discriminate in any way against particular nations or people."

My mother and I came to Texas when I was fourteen years old. I remember my first days in middle school were so hard. This was the first time I really encountered prejudice and racism. One day during lunch, I was sitting down with a group of girls that I wanted to establish a friendship with when suddenly I was harassed by one American girl who presumed I was an illegal Mexican. With deep roots in the United States, I felt this presumption like it was a betrayal. I became ashamed of my Mexican heritage, fearful that I would not be accepted by others. I often told people I was born in California. I've been here since I was ten months old, and my first steps were on American soil. This is the country I call home.

Once I was grown and raising my own family, I lived in constant fear of being torn apart from my children's father, who was undocumented.

On July 8, 2013, our luggage packed, we were leaving for a two-day trip starting at a water park that morning. I went outside to water my plants when I saw my children's dad driving up the driveway. I also noticed a car pulling up right behind him. My worst fear was coming true!

It was ICE. They got out of their car before my husband could even park. ICE surrounded his car, pointing guns at him and shouting to get out with his hands up. That's when I had my first ever panic attack—my heart began beating so hard and fast I thought it was a nightmare. My four kids came out from the house and watched ICE agents take their father into custody and detention. I was horrified and felt hopeless and uncertain. I wanted to comfort my children, but I also wanted to run to their father, like somehow, if I could get to him, we could go back to before this terrifying moment, and everything would be fine.

But he was taken from us, and we were left broken-hearted with a van full of luggage for a trip we couldn't take. They deported my husband to Mexico, and I was left with a full house to support and a welding business to run. Sometimes I felt like giving up because it was just too much to handle. But I found strength in the Lord to continue and never give up.

Any real relationship with my children's father ended because I had to make a really hard decision, the hardest decision. My kids' future had to be my priority, and they would have a better and safer life here. To live in Mexico would greatly reduce their educational opportunities and increase the risk to their lives due to the problems many are facing in Mexico today—human trafficking, organized crime, fighting, drug-related violence, and unlawful killings of civilians.

Nothing is more heartbreaking than to live with the crippling fear of losing a parent to deportation and having your family ripped apart. My children lived through this once. They knew extreme hardship because of it, and it's why the words of their classmates were not just words but felt like real, terrifying threats.

The night of the 2016 presidential election, we were all so anxious to know the outcome. It was getting very late, so I told my children to go to sleep even though I could sense fear all over them. The next morning, my children's first question was "Who is our new president?" rather than the usual "Mom, what's for breakfast?"

I remember how scared they were to go to school that day. Students at my son's school began to talk about how Trump was going to get rid of all the Mexicans. My son told me that most of the Hispanic students stayed quiet. People began to frequently say racist comments in schools and other public places, usually going unchallenged. Two white men approached me in the street during the "Day Without Immigrants" protest, pressing me with questions, asking, "Why don't Mexicans work hard in their own country? Why don't they just wait in line to come here legally like everyone else? Why support foreigners when millions of Americans are unable to find work?"

If entering the US legally was a possibility, we would have done so without hesitation! No one chooses to spend years hiding in the shadows, living each day never knowing what terror tomorrow holds unless that's the only choice left. Despite common misconceptions, entering the country legally is next to impossible. We have limited options for a pathway to citizenship for undocumented workers. I, myself, have been waiting in line for over 20 years for my immigration interview.

It's easy to judge people in a situation that you have never faced or to form an opinion on an issue when it does not directly affect you or your family. Imagine if I were judged instead on the strength I found to run a business, raise my kids, and make a life.

In the Old Testament of the Bible, we can find numerous scriptures where God was very specific to the Israelites about how to treat foreigners. In Deuteronomy 10:18–19 (New International Version), it reads: "He defends the cause of the fatherless and the widow and loves the foreigner residing among you, giving them food and clothing. And you are to love those who are foreigners, for you yourselves were foreigners in Egypt."

Love. Not harass or terrorize. Not even tolerate. The Bible tells Christians that the Lord is loving and compassionate toward all he has made. And we are to be like the Lord. We must reflect on God's love and will. I pray for a change for the lives of millions working to build a life in the land we can call home.

Over time, I stopped living in fear and let myself feel more and more pride in my Mexican heritage. I taught my children to be proud of their history. They are proud of their Mexican heritage. Shouldn't we all be proud of our heritage? Shouldn't we all have a chance to pursue the American dream?

I am a dreamer, and I'm here to stay; I'm here to pursue the American dream! I pray for a change for the lives of millions working to build a life in the land we call home.

JESÚS SALCIDO

"I felt like I came out of the shadows.

I was like a new person. Ever since that day,
I felt like I regained my pride."

—JESÚS SALCIDO

I was born in Chihuahua, Mexico, when my mom and dad were just 16 years old. When I was seven, they decided to move to the United States. All they ever said about it was that they wanted to pursue a better life together. Much later, I found out the real reason. My dad had always wanted to be a cop, just like his grandfather, so he joined the police force at age 18. In Chihuahua, there was a lot of cartel activity, so my dad faced a lot of scary threats. It got to the point where he didn't feel comfortable being out in public with us at the park without having a gun on him. Then my dad was released from the force after suffering two separate breaks in his legs. At that time, my parents were in their early 20s. They still had their whole lives ahead of them. So, they took the risk to head north.

We crossed into the United States on a passenger bus with tourist visas. We didn't have anything, just some clothes, a toy, and a blanket for my sister and me. Soon after arriving, we moved to Fort Worth, Texas. I tried to make the best out of our situation. Even at seven years old, I remember thinking, "I need to hide who I am so I can fit in. That's the best thing that I can do. I need to make sure that people do not know that I am an undocumented immigrant from Mexico. No teachers, no classmates, no friends, nobody should know." That was my secret that I had to keep hidden.

After we moved into a cramped apartment, I was enrolled in school. I struggled because I didn't know any English, and there was no ESL program. I didn't understand anything, and kids would make fun of me. We didn't have a car, so we had to walk miles to school. It was so tiring. But that's the one thing that my parents always ingrained in me: education. "You can always move forward with education," they would say.

I didn't want to be in the United States. If it were up to me, I would have stayed in Mexico. But no one asks a seven-year-old what to do, so those decisions were out of my control.

I worked so hard to master the English language. I remember thinking, "I need to get rid of any accent that I have. While speaking English, nobody can suspect anything. No one can know that I'm from a foreign country, from Mexico." To do this, I would spend my time watching English TV. I also read. I read so much to master the language.

Watching the local Spanish news as a kid taught me everything I know about immigration. They talked about immigration news, things that were going on. They constantly reported on deportations under President Bush. I remember when Texas stopped giving out driver's licenses to undocumented immigrants, and I remember how upset it made my dad.

That's really when my deep fear of the police started. My dad had grown up wanting to be a cop, but I was scared of them because I knew my dad could get pulled over and be deported for having no driver's license. A crippling fear of the police took over my life. They could decide to take advantage of any small mistake or just decide to pull us over and turn us over to ICE. One time when I was out with my dad, he pointed at a van and said, "That's an ICE van. Always be on the lookout for those vans. Always be vigilant."

Every Saturday, the news had an immigration attorney live on the show. People would call in and ask questions. Like many other immigrant children or children of immigrants, I became my family's attorney. I had to fill in and translate everything from apartment leases to school documents, even bank paperwork, and any mail. I had to call the apartment maintenance on behalf of my parents if something was wrong. I had to call DirectTV whenever they were charging us extra or there was something on the bill that didn't make sense to my parents. I had to call Wells Fargo when they were scamming us out of money. It was super stressful for an eight-year-old. I was just a kid constantly dealing with adults who did not take me seriously. I started feeling a lot of resentment toward my parents for making me do that, and school started becoming my sanctuary. It was a place where I was beginning to fit in and make friends now that I knew English.

I became more comfortable as I grew older. By middle school, I had the whole act mastered. I would claim Fort Worth as my hometown. I thought, "Maybe I belong now." That's really all I ever wanted—to be a normal kid and lead a normal life. To be at ease, I lied to myself. I still had that dirty secret that I was undocumented. I still lived with the fear, but I was very good at hiding the fear, too.

Fast forward to high school, and you'd think I was thriving. I was on the soccer team, did theater, and was elected class president. I had friends! I did well academically—I was near the top of my class. Despite all of this, I could only run away so much from being undocumented. By the time my friends were sixteen and seventeen, they started to get driver's licenses and part-time jobs. They filled out their FAFSA applications and applied to colleges and scholarships. They would always ask me, "Hey, why aren't you applying? Why don't you have a car? Why don't you drive? Why don't you have some part-time work so that you can start earning some money?" So, along with my ability to hide my secret and my fear, I became good at making up excuses.

Foolishly, I thought that I could somehow get help to get into college. I would go online to search for applications and scholarships, but every one of them shared a requirement: US permanent residence or US citizenship. I even tried filling out the FAFSA once, and I remember seeing the words "It is a federal crime to turn this in if you are not eligible." All of this was extremely discouraging because I couldn't legally do anything my friends could do. I couldn't move forward with life the way they were moving forward. Frustration piled up inside me. I didn't bust my butt studying, doing homework, and pursuing education only to break my back working construction or in a restaurant. I didn't stay up working on projects only to be blocked from following my heart or my dreams. All I wanted was to go to college and make my family proud.

But even after all that work, not just for school but the constant work to hide my secret and my fear, I still didn't belong. Worse, it was like I didn't really exist. I didn't have any documents—no valid IDs, no social security number. I didn't have a way forward.

My senior year of high school was difficult. I visited the University of Texas (UT), hoping there was a way. I liked the campus, but deep down, I knew I had no shot of getting in because of my secret. I was so stressed talking to an admissions counselor that I broke down in tears. The pressure of hiding since I was seven became too much, and I confessed to a stranger that I was undocumented. I said, "I'm undocumented, and I don't know what to do." That was the first time that I told anybody.

Luckily, there was a sort of loophole at UT. Now I know that it's House Bill 1403. It allowed me to be admitted as an international student to UT, but I would have to sign an affidavit that I lived in Texas so I would qualify for in-state tuition. It bought me four more years, some happiness, and some hope. Maybe I could figure things out during that time. Maybe the Obama administration would do something.

It turned out that college was the hardest time of all. I had to pay my rent because my parents couldn't afford to support me. During the summers, I would work with my dad's friend, remodeling houses and building fences outside in the blistering Texas summer heat. Then I worked at a pillow factory located in a warehouse with no air conditioning. At nineteen, I worked sixty-plus hours a week for low wages just to try to save money to live while I was going to school. I was exhausted.

Because of housing costs, I didn't have the money to pay rent for one semester, so I had to drive three hours back and forth to go to school.

Two years of college passed. I continued my life without telling anybody. I went back to keeping the secret. And I still lived in fear. Then Donald Trump got elected president, and I went to sleep in tears. Two days later, I was in class, and all we did was vent. We didn't do any lectures. After a while of listening to the concerns of the class, nobody had mentioned anything about immigration. I finally blurted out, "I'm scared for my people." My professor responded, "Who are they?" I said, "People like my parents and me who are undocumented." The whole class felt so awkward and uncomfortable after I said that. Nobody said anything else. I felt betrayed in a way because they were supposed to be my UT brethren. We were supposed to be there for each other. Even after all these years, I knew that I still didn't belong, but this time I didn't care.

I felt like I came out of the shadows. I was like a new person. Ever since that day, I felt like I regained my pride. Now I tell stories of my people, making hip-hop music in my language for my people.

Seventeen years have passed since I came to this country, and unfortunately, nothing has changed for immigrants. If anything, things are getting worse. Immigrants are literally feeding the country, taking on even more risk and exposure during the pandemic. We are essential workers, yet we are still terrorized, still locked up in cages and in detention centers, still being separated from our families, still being deported.

I love storytelling with my music. I love bringing stories out of the shadows. But action is just as important. More action needs to be taken by state legislatures and Congress, but also by those of us living in the shadows, everyone living with shadows. It's time to abolish ICE. It's time to create a pathway to citizenship. It's time to dismantle white supremacy and systemic racism in the immigration system and everywhere. It's time to stop living in fear.

SANDRA GARCÍA

"Many families have no idea of the work that gets done so that we have food in the stores and on our tables at home.

We owe a lot to our farmworkers."

—SANDRA GARCÍA

Sometimes I go on a car ride, and I hear a song from Juan Gabriel on the radio. It makes me—oh my gosh—it makes me so sad because I think of my little sister Elsa when she was so young.

She was seven or eight years old when she would sing to us while we were working in the fields. Elsa would charge us twenty-five cents a song and then walk and sing behind the person who requested the song. When the song ended, or she got tired, she would just sit in the middle of the field and wait for us to come back. I don't know how she memorized all those songs that we loved. She still loves to sing.

Both of my parents, my younger sister Susy, and I were born in Mexico. I was a farmworker alongside them for nine years. I think back on how hard it had to be for my parents to see Elsa and my brother out there in the heat for ten hours a day. But my dad would say to us, "Don't ever be embarrassed by who you are. Tell people all the places that you visited. Tell them you've been to Colorado, Montana, and Michigan. Just don't tell them that you went out there working the fields." I guess he thought we would be embarrassed, and maybe other people thought we should be embarrassed. But we were not.

We worked in Colorado and Montana for several years but spent most of our summers in Michigan. We also worked in West Texas. The schedule was six days a week for ten hours a day. I remember praying for rain, even though my parents didn't like rain because we wouldn't get paid. But it was a little break for us. The moment dark clouds would appear, we kids would start praying (quietly). The work raised many blisters on our hands, and after they popped, we would continue working. We also ended up with major sunburns. Six days a week were for work in the fields, and Sundays were for church, the laundromat, and grocery shopping.

We were children. It was a lot of work, but I don't remember complaining. It was just something we had to do to help the family. The money we earned was not for us; it mostly went to fix our house and whatever my parents decided to do with it. I was nine or ten years old when I started working, but they listed me as having thirteen years. Being thirteen meant you got paid as an adult, but it also meant you had to work as hard as an adult.

Of course, my mom and dad were always next to me, helping me. There were also so many good things about all these years. We were always together as a family. I had very good parents who only wanted to give us a better life than what we had in Mexico. In Mexico, we lived on a ranch with no electricity and no running water. Today, I can't imagine my kids working ten hours a day, doing hard labor, and all the while in the sun. But somehow, my family did it.

We worked on sugar beets, beans, cherries, corn, and cucumbers. Cucumbers are one of the worst jobs ever. The first couple of days on cucumbers is extremely painful. Your back hurts so much. I remember my mother would help me by pushing my body down so I could sit on the toilet. But then my body would get used to it, and we would continue working until there was no more picking or until school was about to start, and we had to return back home to Texas.

Every time I go grocery shopping, I can't help but think of all the people who worked so hard so that I can go into a store and shop for my fruits and vegetables. I think of all the little hands. Many families have no idea of the work that gets done, so that we have food in the stores and on our tables at home. We owe a lot to our farmworkers. Every time I pick out a cucumber at the grocery store, I swear to God my back hurts. I swear I feel it, and I remember my poor mother and what she had to do when we could not sit on the toilet. Don't get me wrong; I still love to eat cucumbers.

Being a farmworker, you don't get treated like a human being. People see you as being beneath them. While working in Montana, I remember a truck driving by, and someone calling us whores. It was my mother, my two aunts, my sister, and myself. And I was like, "whores?" I didn't understand why those men called us that! We were just working. We were doing something good, something important, yet farmworkers just don't get the respect they deserve. Many times while we worked the fields, farmers would spray pesticides right there next to us. The airplanes would fly over us with no consideration for our being there.

Another awful thing that we had to deal with was the bathrooms. Bathrooms were never, ever provided. My husband and I flip homes for a living now, and the first thing that we do is provide a portable toilet on site. But for us working in the field, there was nothing. It was an open field, so without a bathroom, there was no privacy. Can you imagine how horrible it was being a girl and being on your period? It was the worst. We would get so excited when we would see corn fields next to any fields we were to be working on. Corn grows tall. Even now, when I pass corn fields, I still remember that good feeling of relief we would all get.

There was also a farmer in Michigan whom I will never forget. His name was Carl. We worked for him for many years. One day Carl told me to ask my dad how much money my dad would want for purchasing me. When I told my dad, he got so upset. I remember him saying, "We are never going to work for him again! Who the hell does he think he is?!" Carl came to the fields the next day, and I just told him, "I'm not for sale." You see, my parents didn't speak English, and I was the oldest, so I was their interpreter. I don't think I really understood at the time; how could he think I was for sale? Would he have asked his neighbor if he could buy their child? What made him think I was for sale?

There was also a farmer in Montana who placed us in a home that was right next to the cows. We thought it was great until we realized we were going to share the house with tons of ticks. They were all over the house! We would stick cotton balls in our ears so that the ticks didn't go inside. That's what the farmer gave us, and we lived like that all summer long. We didn't have a choice.

Prior to being farmworkers, my parents, my sister, and I lived illegally in East Texas and San Antonio. I was little, and I remember always living in fear. I wasn't quite sure of what, but I remember being scared. I remember looking through the windows, not sure what to look for but because that's what my parents would do. I remember living in a garage with my parents and other adults related to my parents. We all slept on the floor. One day while my dad was working in Lufkin, immigration picked him up and sent us back to Mexico. It wasn't hard for us to cross the river again because we lived right next to it. We used to cross it for fun. And then one day we came back to the United States, but as resident aliens. That's when we were placed in a school where I didn't speak their language. I don't know how we managed to pass grades because it was hard, and we had no one at home to help.

We were never in any trouble. We never did anything illegal. We just worked hard, and when we got back home from working all summer, we went straight to school. If I wanted to go to the movies or a dance, I would work on the weekends when there was picking to do. I would get on a bus in my hometown of Eagle Pass with a whole bunch of men and leave town at five in the morning. I left home for Austin at the age of eighteen. I wasn't too scared of not making it. I knew how to work hard, and I knew I would not starve.

My dad used to always say, "Never, ever, ever marry a farmworker. They will bring you back. No, you guys need to study." He told his four daughters and one son whom he had raised while working the fields, "Y'all need to study, and you need to get an education. Don't ever, ever come back over here. This is not what you want to do with your life. Study so that you never come back." I know he always felt sorry for taking us to work.

My sisters have graduated from St. Edwards and University of Texas, and we have all done well. It has helped us a lot to understand the value of hard work. Not everyone does. My dad says he is very proud of us. My mom has passed away, but I know my mom was proud of us, too. We are who we are because of them.

My parents became US citizens many years ago. They would ask me, "Why don't you become a US citizen?" My response was always, "Why do I have to pay? They should give it to me. I've been reporting on my social security ever since I can remember, I've never been arrested, I don't even have any tickets, I worked for the state government all my adult career, and I still have to pay?" I couldn't understand for so long. Like many people, I got stuck on the money. Now I think it was dumb of me to think that way.

I am now a US citizen, and I can vote!

In the winter before the COVID-19 pandemic, I was talking to my sisters about wanting to rent a house and take my kids to work the fields for the entire summer. I offered to take their kids as well, and they liked the idea. I knew the work would kill my back, but I wanted them to know what it takes to work in the fields, to appreciate what these people are doing for us and for our country. I wanted my children to understand, to humble themselves, even if, more than likely, they would get discriminated against. I wanted them to know what farmworkers do and be an advocate for them one day. Then the virus came in and messed up my plans. But I'm still thinking of taking them one of these days. I'm going to rent a house somewhere, and I'm going to take my kids and the kids of anyone else who wants to send them. I want them to know what it feels like to feed America.

ÁNGEL PIEDRAS

"I always hear how we Mexicans are accused of being criminals, but I was able to see very closely all the corruption that exists on the US side of the border, too."

—ÁNGEL PIEDRAS

In my heart, there was a mix of sadness and excitement—sadness because I was leaving everything behind, and excitement because I knew that I was going to be able to find work and help my family.

I was thirteen years old when I set foot on American soil, and I have been here ever since. This is where my home is. This is where my wife and my children are. Like many immigrants before me, I came seeking work. I'm from a small ranch in Mexico, and for people like us, there is no work. I needed to work to help my parents.

Two weeks after being here, I wanted to go back, but when I started working, I loved it. I liked the money that I earned, so I started working hard to earn more money. I would send more than $1,000 monthly to help my parents because there were fourteen of us siblings. With the money, my parents were able to remodel their home, which was very old, deteriorated, and badly in need of repairs. I didn't spend any of the money I earned on myself.

I attended high school in the evenings because I was working all day long. I arrived at school feeling very tired. Maybe that was the reason I didn't learn English very well. After I got married, I continued sending money to my parents, though it was less. Then my wife and I had three children. All of them were born in this country, so they are all American citizens. That's when everything changed for me because I became focused on my little family. Of course, this meant there were many more bills to pay, too.

I worked in construction, on everything involved in remodeling: sheetrock, framing, doors, painting, texture, roofs, etc. I learned to do it all, to do quality work. I would get off construction work at 3:30 p.m., so I looked for a job in a restaurant. At the restaurant, I started work at 4:00 p.m. and finished at 12:30 a.m., so I didn't get home until 1:30 a.m. Then I had to wake up at 5:00 a.m. I barely had time to sleep. That was my daily routine, and I kept at it for more than two years.

I also learned about mechanics and was able to fix my own cars. I did this to save money, so we didn't have to pay mechanics to fix our cars. On a Tuesday morning at 11:45 a.m., I went to comply with the inspection requirements so that I wouldn't have any problems with the authorities. They gave me a piece of paper, and I went to the sheriff's office to get the sticker. When I got out, I called my wife, telling her that I was on my way home. Five minutes after I spoke with her, I was stopped by a police officer. He said his reason for stopping me was that my window tints were too dark. I showed him the paper that had my car's inspection and told him that they didn't mention this on the report. I was carrying the insurance policy and my passport as a document of identification. What I wasn't carrying with me was a driver's license. The reason I didn't have a license is that I am an undocumented immigrant, and the laws don't allow us to qualify for one, even though we desperately need it.

So, I had nothing else to show him. Because of this, he arrested me. He took me to jail like a criminal. After I was detained, the ICE officers came for me and moved me to the detention center in Pearsall, Texas, for seven months. We paid a lot of money for lawyers to fight the case, but we lost. With everything that happened, I became depressed. I felt impotent, knowing that my family was out there needing me. I was the sole provider for my family, and wondering how they were going to survive without me tortured me.

I witnessed other inmates trying to commit suicide. Some around me would cut their own veins. Some went to the restroom to try to hang themselves, or sometimes they would jump from the beds that are six feet high, trying to commit suicide. Many died from COVID. I would see them being carried on stretchers, and they would not come back. The guards didn't want us looking in the halls at all of these things, and they would also turn off our TVs so that we couldn't watch the news.

Inmates were separated by different uniforms. The ones in blue were on their first offense and were on the list to be deported. The ones in orange were there because they had a second offense, but somehow they were able to get out on bail for $8,000 or $10,000. I did not understand why those with two offenses could get out more easily than those of us who only had one offense.

I tried to keep myself busy. I applied for a job at the detention center and started doing janitorial work for $1 a day. Then, I found out that in the kitchen, they paid more—$3 a day—so I applied there and then did laundry, where they also paid $3 a day. The phone calls out of the detention center had a horrible connection and were extremely expensive—one minute cost $2—but I needed to be in contact with my family and my wife.

Then the day arrived when they deported me. None of the efforts of my wife, her activism, and all the legal fees we had spent mattered. I was deported to the Laredo border, and to my surprise, we were received on the Mexican side by the military dressed up as civilians. They took us to a shelter called "the house of the immigrant." Once there, they offered us a bus service to take us to our destination, but while we were waiting for the bus, we were kidnapped by members of organized crime (drug cartels), who took us to a home where there were other people who had been deported like me.

We were imprisoned in that house, separated into different rooms. I could hear women and children. Because we were in the hands of organized crime, I thought that they were simply going to kill us. We weren't allowed to talk to anybody, except for extortion purposes, to ask for money from our relatives so that they could free us. They wanted a ransom of $10,000 per person. Besides that amount, I would also need to "purchase" what they called a warrant for $4,000 more, which they said would allow me to continue my travels all the way to Mexico City, where my parents lived.

My wife was in anguish. She had to get two loans to come up with the ransom money. This is on top of all the lawyers' fees incurred while I was detained. She got into so much debt. I was held in that place for two entire days, and those have been the longest two days of my life. That is the place where I was the most scared I have ever been in my life. That was the time that I prayed to God the most in my entire life.

When they finally set me free, they took me to the bus station. When my family picked me up in Mexico City, my father had just passed away. As two months passed, I took advantage of the opportunity to spend time with my family, whom I hadn't seen for more than fourteen years. I worked on my parents' home, using the skills I had learned to make some improvements that were desperately needed. Still, I lived in misery after everything I had been through and being so far away from my wife and children. I was desperate to find a way to get home to them.

After thinking everything through, I decided to look for a coyote who would help me cross the border. I found one whose fees were $8,500. You have to pay for what they call a "permit," which is a code provided by the cartel. The code allowed us to cross the border without organized crime interfering or touching us. With this, we crossed the river with the coyote in plain daylight at eleven o'clock. There were twenty-two people in the group and three guides swimming across.

We got to a tunnel, and the Border Patrol officers were right there. They saw us, but they pretended they didn't. Later, the coyote revealed to me that the Border Patrol officers received $1,000 for each of us who crossed the border in that group.

I always hear how we Mexicans are accused of being criminals, but I was able to see very closely all the corruption that exists on the US side of the border, too. Those Border Patrol officers work alongside the coyotes and organized crime groups. They are accomplices. Who knows how many offenses they have committed?

Next, there was a group waiting for us in a jeep. They took us to a house, divided the group in two, and put us in two trucks, but before reaching the checkpoints, we had to get out of the trucks and walk. We walked from 7.00 p.m. until 3.00 p.m. the next day. Then we headed towards our final destinations in different parts of Texas. Everything seems like a nightmare. In less than a year, I was detained because of the window tint of my car. I was in jail, deported, kidnapped, and then I took the biggest risk of all in order to be reunited with my family.

This has been a traumatic experience, but also a learning process. I was able to experience another reality that people don't see; what happens inside the detention centers, how the immigration system is racist and unjust, and the corruption of authorities at all levels and on both sides of the border.

Here I am, reunited with my wife and children. I can still picture them crying with joy when they first saw me. Everything that I did, I did it for them. I came back, taking on all the risks that involved. Yet, if I am stopped by a police officer, at his discretion, he can do the same thing to me all over again.

I have always done whatever I could for my family, from the first time that I set foot in this country. From that moment, it has become my home, where my three US citizen children now live. They don't deserve to grow up without their father. I will always do whatever I can to offer them a better life and a better future.

ÁNGEL PIEDRAS

CARMEN ZUVIETA

"My children had the right to have their father in their lives. I wasn't going to allow a broken system to snatch their father away from them."

—CARMEN ZUVIETA

When I became pregnant with my first son, it woke up in me an impulse to protect both him and myself. Through the years, this impulse of protection has extended to the powerless as well.

I come from a small village where there was no electricity at all. I am the daughter of illiterate farmers. My father attended elementary school until the third grade but was a very smart man. My mother was completely illiterate. I am the first of nine siblings, and consequently, I was a second mother to all of them. I left my village for the first time when I was twelve years old, and that was also my first time seeing vehicles and television. At that young age, I went to work in another village that was about eight hours away from my home. My job was to clean houses as a maid, living in the home where I worked. At night, I studied for high school.

I lived in an environment of domestic violence and psychological, verbal, and sexual abuse. So when I turned sixteen, I moved to the United States. When I got pregnant, I found it very difficult to work with my son, so I came back to my family in Mexico. Back in Mexico, I met my now husband of twenty-five years. During that time, the North American Free Trade Agreement (NAFTA) between the US and Mexico had just been implemented, and agriculture essentially lost its value. This left farmers without jobs, so many of them came to the US looking for work, including my family.

In 2001, my husband had his first incident with the authorities. Years later, in 2008, he was detained and was arrested for this past incident. During that time, the Secure Communities program *(comunidades seguras)* was in effect, which meant that there was an alliance between the police and immigration authorities such that if someone was arrested, the police were obligated to transfer undocumented immigrants to immigration authorities immediately.

My husband was transferred to immigration detention. This is where my struggle with the unjust immigration system begins. I promised him that I was going to fight for him until my last breath.

When everything seemed impossible, I was able to get him out on bail. I hired lawyers, fought in court, and appealed, but every appeal was denied. Still, it was not a waste, and I was not finished fighting. Through all this, I was trying to buy time while processing my green card application, and with my two children, who are US citizens, I was hopeful for a change in immigration laws.

During this process and in between court appointments, I became pregnant with my youngest son; at the same time, my middle daughter was diagnosed with diabetes. This was a very stressful time in my life. I remember the judge asking me: "Why don't you all leave for Mexico?" I responded that my children were American citizens, that they had the right to live in this country. Besides, with my daughter's complete dependence on insulin, I couldn't risk her health. I had an acquaintance from Mexico whose kids had been diagnosed with diabetes, the same type as my daughter, and one of them had died because of lack of proper care. This tragedy was always in the back of my mind. My daughter was an American citizen, and she didn't qualify for any type of health care back in Mexico. I wasn't willing to expose my children to this harsh reality and take away from them their right to live in this country.

At that moment in court, I decided to stay in this country and to fight for them with everything that I had. The lawyer told me that I was the person who could help the most in my husband's case, even though I was undocumented as well. I fought and risked everything I had. In 2013, my daughter, struggling with her diabetes and on the verge of losing her father to unjust laws, fell into a severe depression, attempted suicide, and had to be hospitalized.

I felt enormous pressure. My husband's fight was not just his fight, and not just my fight, but a severe oppression weighing on my children. By this time, I had become part of an activist organization. I knew my rights, and I was exploring the legal options I had to continue fighting for my husband. The activist organization, as well as a church that I was part of, helped me a great deal in gathering and sending five hundred letters and faxes. It was during this time that I received my green card.

On February 18, my daughter was finally released from the hospital, and on the next day, my husband had his court appointment in San Antonio. Even though he was complying with everything that was required of him, on that very day he was unexpectedly taken away and deported to Mexico. My husband called me from the Mexican border at midnight to tell me that he had been deported. I had still been fighting his case, trying to find out where they had detained him to pressure the authorities with the help of activist organizations. But it turned out to be pointless because they had already deported him to Mexico, and there was nothing that we could do about it. He told me to take care of our children, that I was a good woman and that I could handle it all.

My husband told me to either rent or sell the house because I wouldn't be able to handle all the home expenses alone. He told me not to spend any more money to hire lawyers or on anything that had to do with him because it was too much money. He wasn't willing to cross the border illegally again because he didn't want to risk going back to jail. So, he stayed in Mexico, separated from his wife and children against his will.

I renewed my promise to him that it didn't matter how long it took me; I was going to fight for him until my last breath if he also decided to fight this with me. My children had the right to have their father in their lives. I wasn't going to allow a broken system to snatch their father away from them. Unable to take the risk, he hadn't seen his own parents or family in more than fifteen years.

My youngest son would search for his dad inside his truck. Other days, he would hear the door to the house open and think it was his dad coming back home. Eventually, my son stopped talking. My daughter's depression grew worse. We were facing very difficult times.

I continued working and growing in activism. This is how I discovered that the Secure Communities program facilitated taking my husband away from us. I wanted to take down that program so that other families and other children wouldn't experience what our family was going through, suffering separation, and all the effects it can have on physical and psychological health. I organized against the county and its participation in the Secure Communities program, asking the sheriff to stop participating in it.

I submitted my husband's legal application, and the lawyer told me that it would take a very long time, that it could be five or ten years. I told him that I didn't care; we had to go on. In the activist organization that I had become a part of, there was a lawyer who helped me submit a Freedom of Information Act request, and through this, we discovered that the sheriff was having conversations with US Citizenship and Immigration Services, investigating my life and my case to find a way to attack me. That didn't stop me either.

Years went by, and election season came again. We started working with the sheriff candidates, organizing forums, and asking questions about the Secure Communities program. When a new sheriff, Sally Hernandez, was elected, she kept her promise during community conversations to get rid of the program. This caused the governor to retaliate against her and take away some of her funding.

Next, I visited several legislators and talked to them about my personal case and about my community, because my case was a mirror for many families who, unlike myself, felt intimidated and remained quiet. I visited the offices of Senator Ted Cruz and then-Speaker of the House John Boehner.

Two years went by, and my husband was still in Mexico. His first application for residency was rejected. Of course, I continued. If they rejected a case, I opened another one. I wasn't giving up. I was keeping my promise. I found ways to work on his case with lawyers, and we decided to present his paperwork for the State Department's pardon petitions. After another year and a half, we obtained those pardons. But the most stressful part was still to come: interviews with the judge.

Throughout these four years, my life was work, children, and activism. I had no room for anything else. Every three months, we would go to the border to see my husband, crossing in Laredo. He had to ride the bus for twelve hours to be able to see his children for too little time. I spent a total of $30,000 in legal fees, including government fees and lawyers' fees.

What did I achieve during this time? I was able to make my voice heard. I saw the power of change, the power of the community, and the value of alliances. I learned to assert my rights and my children's rights. I learned to resist, to persist, to never give up in all areas of my life. I saw how many voices are silenced by unjust authorities, and that far too many choose to be silent even when they can see another being oppressed. I think that is the worst thing that you can do, to be silent in the face of injustice. It doesn't make sense to simply be an inhabitant of this world; to me, a true citizen means to seek justice, to be in solidarity with the community, to seek the good of others, and to fight the idea that any authority should decide which children have the right to be with their parents and which ones don't.

My representative gave me a letter supporting my husband's return. I also got a letter from the mayor asking that no more families be separated. Finally, they gave him the immigration appointment we were waiting for, and our whole family was in the hands of one person who, entirely at their own discretion, would decide the future of my husband and of our whole family.

On December 13, my husband got out of the immigration office, and he was so stressed and overwhelmed that he didn't exactly know what had just happened. He said that he was told that he would receive his papers by mail. I looked at the paper in his hand, and it said that within fifteen business days, he would get his cherished papers.

We had finally won.

I was hoping that this was the last Christmas that we would spend apart. But miracles occur, and he received his documents on December 22, which happens to be my birthday. The next day, he got on the bus and arrived just in time for us to celebrate Christmas 2017 together as a family.

I kept my promise to him that I would fight until my last breath. It took a lot of patience and endurance. I don't think many marriages would survive being apart for four years, but we did it. In the end, I discovered that true love is to forget about myself and to help others. Now my voice has also become the voice of others. Everything I've learned, I use to help others who are going through similar situations.

I don't know if I'll ever get to see it, but I will keep fighting for true justice. I am sowing seeds right now, and my hope is that someone else can reap the fruit of what I've sown. If I die tomorrow, I will tell God that I tried to fulfill my mission in this world. I will have left a legacy to my children, an example of being a fighter and of not giving up. It's up to them to either follow my lead or allow someone to step over them.

ADRIÁN ZAMORA

"I started spotting opportunities instead of barriers; it was a mental change that has stuck with me since."

—ADRIÁN ZAMORA

I remember asking my World Studies teacher, Ms. Lemke, if it was even worth applying to college, knowing I was not going to qualify for FAFSA, knowing that I did not qualify for a majority of the scholarships out there, knowing that my parents would not be able to afford it, and knowing that I was undocumented. It was the first time I had told any adult at my high school about my reality, and I felt very vulnerable. My thoughts were racing at the anticipation of her response: "Why did I ask her that? Will she see me differently now? How will this affect our relationship? Will she tell the principal? Will I get in trouble?"

She closed the door to her classroom during her study hour to discuss my situation and empathized with my reality. "I had no idea about your past, and I appreciate your trust in me. I know there's a lot of ambiguity and precautions that you have to take and will continue to take as you progress in life. But I know that you are a curious kid, you aren't just smart; you excel in groups, you lead the class discussions, and those qualities will morph into your key strengths one day. It will be difficult, but don't limit your dreams in life by the cards you were dealt with from the start." From then on, I started spotting opportunities instead of barriers; it was a mental change that has stuck with me since.

My parents brought me to the US from Durango, Mexico, at the age of four. They took care of me as best as they could, always putting my education above everything else. I was put into a bilingual school at first so I could adjust to English, but as soon as my mom saw that I was not picking it up fast enough, she threw me in the deep end and transferred me to a mostly white elementary school called Bryker Woods. I learned English within six months, and before I knew it, I was translating everything for my parents, from their taxes to dentist appointments and teacher evaluations (although I took the liberty to refrain from telling them everything on those).

One of my earliest memories was finding out that my mother needed surgery on her ear due to a horrible treatment she got back in the rural town we were from. She had an ear infection as a girl that was treated with a water syringe. It was done poorly with more pressure than the human ear drums could handle, and she had lost most of her hearing on her left ear since then. I remember speaking with the financial operator about her insurance. "No insurance," I'd said with my limited English. As undocumented immigrants, we front the full cost for any medical treatment we get since we do not qualify for insurance, even though most of us can afford it. My mother needed this operation done decades ago, but after receiving the quote for the total bill, she didn't want to burden the family any longer and decided not to go through with it.

Shortly after, my brother was born here in Austin, Texas, and I was the happiest brother alive just for that day. Later I found out that my mother had again sacrificed comfort to lessen the burden of the bill for my father: she had my brother without any anesthetics. It was obvious to me from a young age that huge disparities plagued the undocumented community.

As my family assimilated to the United States, my dad began teaching my mom how to drive. They grew up in different times, and my grandfather never taught his daughters how to drive. I remember her telling me that she was pulled from middle school to fulfill her duties at home. It was a different time for sure, but my mom was eager to learn, and I remember for four years straight, she would only take Lamar Boulevard to our school because she was afraid of the highway. When she got her license, I was so happy and proud of her. Now she had a valid ID and did not have to drive in fear any longer. That only lasted for a decade or so because around ten years ago, a new law was passed stating that no one without a social security number could receive a license.

This law would change the lives of hundreds of thousands of people who would never get the opportunity to learn how to drive safely as my parents did. The law would immediately label them as criminals subject to a citation at best and deportation at worst. Assimilating to the US would become that much harder, and every time they sat behind the wheel, they would take on a terrible risk. They never knew if the next time they went grocery shopping would be the last, and their children were never sure that their parents would come home. This was meant to be another deterrence for immigrants coming to the United States, but it really is just another way of going around the real problem instead of addressing it.

I remember comparing my upbringing here in the United States to carrying a deadly secret in an action movie, a secret so lethal that if discovered, all the work my parents and I had done to have a normal life would vanish in an instant. My fear was real and had real repercussions in my life. I would not say a word to my closest friends about my status because I did not want them to think any differently of me, and I also did not want to put my family in a risky situation that could be avoided by acting like I was normal, by keeping the secret at all costs. And to this very day, there are many just like me, carrying and hiding this secret of their existence in the wrong place.

Here's an example: I was in the seventh grade, and I thought I had made an awesome friend who really related to me. We had similar hobbies and a lot of the same classes, and he was one of the few friends whom I told about my status.

I blindly put my trust in him to keep it to himself. As soon as the words came out of my mouth, he shouted to the whole class, "Hey everyone, Adrián is an illegal immigrant." I laughed and tried to play it off as best as I could, but I was embarrassed and felt targeted. I knew not to say a word after that, and so I went back into hiding and closed the door on opening up to anyone else, at least at that point in my life.

Or take the second grade for another example: everyone knows that one kid who is a troublemaker, right? I don't know what reason or what problem Nick had that day, but he convinced me to play that game where you open up your hand and try to go in between all of your fingers with your pencil really fast; it sounded fun. He went first, and when I opened my hand, he stabbed me with his pencil. I still have the mark to this day, and the only other memory I have of that kid is when I was jumping rope in P.E. class, and he walked right up to me and called me a "stupid Mexican." I don't think those two events were coincidences or isolated events.

I identified as American but knew that I had no status. I knew the United States' short but rich history better than Mexico's, and at this point, I spoke English better than my native tongue. I needed to figure out a way to pay for college with minimal assistance from my parents. Luckily, I had amazing counselors and teachers who guided me through the process of applying for colleges and scholarships. At the end of the day, I decided to go to Austin Community College because of the financial limitations I had at the time. I had two jobs while at ACC so I could save up to transfer to a four-year university. I got my associates' degree and was off to Texas Tech University on an amazing transfer scholarship that paid for all of my tuition!

In the middle of my junior year at Texas Tech, I received a call telling me that my grandmother had passed away. My mother had moved here when she was twenty-seven and did not see her mother for a decade, at which point my grandmother visited once a year on a tourist visa for the next decade or so. Can you imagine only seeing your mother once a year for the rest of your life after your mid-twenties? It was heartbreaking. I knew I wouldn't be able to go to her funeral, which took a toll on me, but I can't even begin to fathom what my mother was going through. She had packed up her bags the next day and was ready to leave and never come back, but she ended up staying because she knew that my grandmother would want her to fulfill her duty to her children, as any mother would do. Five years later, my mother has still not been able to go and visit her mother at the cemetery to pay her respects. This is just one example of what mothers and fathers sacrifice for their children when they cross the border.

Just like that, after almost being done with college, after completing an internship and receiving a job offer, I was painfully reminded of my barriers. I was okay with working multiple jobs to pay for college, with not being able to study abroad while in college. I was okay with a lot of things, but I never imagined that my mother would have to endure something like that just so she could watch me grow up to be the man I am today.

As we go through life, our brains tend to filter out experiences, memories, or issues that don't really apply to our everyday lives or have a significant impact on our immediate social bubble. It's just a natural human tendency we have that programs us to go into familiar daily cycles. This is why it is hard to be consistent with goals. We are constantly bombarded with information like social media, studying for exams, making plans with friends, etc. Our brain is always trying to figure out what the next thing is, and that cycle of planning competes with looking meaningfully and constructively towards the future. It's one of the reasons big problems that require years to solve often are ignored. Yet, that kind of critical, strategic, future-oriented thinking is a distinction of human consciousness. Think of the plastic in the ocean, for example; we know it's there, we feel guilty about it, possibly a little more during shark week or when we visit a nasty beach, but then when we're back in our homes and we get back into our social bubble, the problem of plastic disappears from our thoughts.

I implore you not to let this happen with immigration and the steps that need to be taken to enable a safer and more educated United States. We all know that it's an ongoing issue, but it might not affect your everyday lives. But it does affect my everyday life and seven hundred thousand other Dreamers who are a subset of the eleven million undocumented immigrants in the United States. We need each other as we are already intertwined economically, socially, politically, and the next person you meet in college or at a fundraising event could be someone who has been in hiding for most of their life. Be the reason they can trust you; educate your peers about the misconceptions about us and what we face; do your research on the plausible solutions and urge your local, state, and federal lawmakers to vote on which ones you think are best.

You are our voice because we don't have one on paper. But you're hearing me now, and I am living proof that someone who didn't speak a lick of English when brought here overcame many of the issues that still need to be tackled nationally.

The college debt crisis? I'm debt-free (it can be done!) Unemployment after college? I was hired into one of the best finance development programs in the world after college. Even so, my barriers are still not gone. When my company's international conference in Singapore was announced, I had the confidence and courage to tell my manager that I could not go because I was a Dreamer. Thankfully, Ms. Lemke wasn't the last person in my life who was open to learning about my past. Throughout college, my career, and even now, I am thankful to share my journey with you.

TONY RUIZ
───────────────

"I know more about football than soccer. I bleed blue for the damn Dodgers, you know? This is my home, this is my very own country, but I am treated like a stranger here."

—TONY RUIZ

My earliest memory is from when I was about three years old and was wearing an apron in the kitchen, like a preview of what my life was going to be like. My parents brought me to this country from Oaxaca, Mexico, when I was only one year old. Of course, I have no memory of that. I know my home state of Oaxaca only through pictures, TV shows, and documentaries. I feel ashamed not to know more about my own people, but I have lived all my life in this country. I went to kindergarten, elementary school, and high school on the west side of Los Angeles. I know more about football than soccer. I bleed blue for the damn Dodgers, you know? This is my home, this is my very own country, but I am treated like a stranger here.

Spanish was my first language, so when I started kindergarten, I took ESL classes and didn't know the difference back then. All the way throughout elementary I managed to make good grades. On the weekends, I helped my mom at the dry cleaner where she was working. Thankfully, her boss allowed her to take me to work because she didn't have anyone to leave me with. So, I helped her put the foam on the hangers. By the end of my elementary years, I started to notice some differences at my mom's work. I noticed that there were people who put foam on the hangers, like my mom and me, while others just dropped off their clothes, and I quickly realized that I wanted to be like those people who dropped things off.

Other times, my dad would pick me up and take me to work with him at the Sandbags Deli in Westwood. I would watch him work, and I would be amazed. He was a seasoned worker, and he was awesome, and I knew that I wanted to be like that. He also taught me how to cook. My work ethic comes from my parents, both hard workers.

Because of my good grades in elementary school, my teacher and my mom wanted me to go to a better middle school than the one I was supposed to go to, so that I could have a better opportunity and to protect me from bad influences, like gangs. They enrolled me in Emerson Middle School with all the white kids who were fortunate to have a good education.

I went from being a top student in elementary to a school where my English wasn't good enough. I couldn't write an essay. I couldn't catch up, and this was a problem because I liked school. I had no support at home because neither of my parents knew anything about it. They were both immigrants and barely spoke English, so how could they even help me? Now, at least there are apps for that, but back then, there was nothing.

I was barely making it in middle school. I had no friends. I tried to make friends, but we had nothing in common. Our cultures and backgrounds were so different. Everything was different: the books that the kids were reading, the materials they were using for their projects. I couldn't keep up with that. I started seeing the separation, the segregation of the honors kids from the regular students like me. Then there were the lunch tickets to get free food, or county tickets, as me and my homies used to call them. I was getting tickets to get lunch while the other kids could get anything they wanted with real money, spending $5 or more for lunch, in Subway, and other places.

I used to love those tickets in elementary, but not in middle school, because now I saw the difference, and it made me ashamed to use them. I felt like whatever I did, I could not level with the other kids. I realized at a young age that there are some things in life that I would have to work extra hard on. I suffered in silence.

All of this changed my view of life. I started really struggling then. I was only eleven years old, and I was experiencing a culture shock in my own country. High school wasn't any better. There was this time in high school where we had the opportunity to go on a trip to Europe, but I couldn't go because I was undocumented and therefore couldn't apply for a passport or any kind of identification. After this, my parents took me to a spot in L.A. called MacArthur Park, a place where they make fake IDs. That's where you need to go when you're undocumented.

When I turned sixteen, I started working at iHOP. My sister worked there as a cashier handling money. I became a server, and I liked the responsibility. I didn't feel the need for education anymore because it was awesome making my own money. After working at iHOP, I went to P.F. Chang's in Santa Monica. I went from the hood to the west part of town, to the white, rich community, and I had to change who I was, the way I dressed, the way I talked, everything to be able to fit in, to become "Caucasian friendly."

It's a different story now because I'm comfortable with who I am. But even though I grew up in this country, I'm not an American on paper.

I was twenty-one when I realized I would probably never get to work in a high-end kitchen because most of them use E-Verify, and I wouldn't pass the background check. That's when even the restaurant world I felt at home in started to make me feel like I didn't belong, and I realized how serious it was not to have papers. It crushed me because I used to dream of someday opening my own restaurant. I have the drive and determination to do it.

I didn't apply for the Deferred Action for Childhood Arrivals (DACA) because I didn't think I needed it. I've done everything in the restaurant business; that's my bread and butter. I had a steady job as a line cook at the San Francisco Saloon, the long-standing bar and grill on Pico Boulevard. But then the pandemic hit, and it has been so hard on the restaurant business. I never imagined something like this would happen. Now I feel like I have to apply for DACA, but it's expensive.

I've been struggling ever since the pandemic shut down the restaurant business. First, we thought it would be two weeks, then a month; then after two and three months went by, we started losing hope. I have not only lost my job to the coronavirus outbreak, but my savings have eroded away as well. Now I'm in crisis mode. I got evicted from the home that I was living in over a dispute involving missed rent, and I find myself scanning Craigslist job boards daily for work, trying not to fall into despair.

I have no access to unemployment benefits or federal, state, or city emergency relief funds because of my status as an undocumented immigrant. These days, I have been surviving with help from family, friends, and coworkers. I put most of my personal belongings in storage and spent the past several nights drifting between families' and friends' houses, sleeping on couches.

Working in the kitchen, cooking, or dishwashing for eight to fourteen hours straight is hard work. It's hot, you get fire in your face, it's competitive, people have attitudes, and it doesn't pay well—about $14.25 per hour. Few people are committed to the job unless they have the passion or the need. The American restaurant industry hinges on the labor of undocumented workers, and many work in low-pay back-of-house jobs without worker protections or access to benefits.

The pandemic exposed how this industry relies on such workers to make restaurants profitable; and they are the most at risk for health issues and hunger. Now the workers who have been making restaurants run efficiently have been left to fend for themselves. The first thing they ask you for on the unemployment website is your social security number. I don't have one. Should I try to buy one at MacArthur Park?

I am thirty-one years old now, and every attempt my parents have made to get me a permanent resident card over the years has failed. It feels like I'm fighting for my life with my hands tied behind my back. The shutdown has opened old wounds for me related to my complicated bicultural identity and place in the world. It has been a vivid reminder of the ways my life has been shaped and how my ambitions have been warped by forces beyond my control.

So what do I do? Just pray that a miracle will happen?

MIRIAM JAIMES

"It didn't matter how smart I was or how good my grades were; I was not allowed to study or work and do what I wanted because of my immigration status."

—MIRIAM JAIMES

I am sitting in the back seat of a car, and my sister is sitting right next to me. A stranger is driving us somewhere. The driver is a woman who I don't know. I don't know what we are doing or where we are going. I don't really know anything about what is happening. All I know is that I am feeling very anxious because my mom and dad are not here with us. The woman stops the car and gives us something; she wants us to take medicine. I think it is Benadryl or something like that. My sister and I obey and drink it.

I don't know all of what happened after that. All I know is that when I opened my eyes, we were in a McDonald's in San Antonio, Texas.

I was born in a small town south of Mexico City called Luvianos, the middle child of three girls. Growing up, I remember having everything we wanted. We had a good economic position, and we had a gorgeous two-story home. When I was eleven years old, my dad came in one day and, out of the blue, told us that we were moving to the US to work. I felt confused. If we had everything we needed and a good and stable economic position, why did we need to go elsewhere for work?

Later in life, I would discover that my dad wasn't telling the whole story. The real reason we needed to leave Mexico was that he was being persecuted by organized crime in Mexico. My dad left first, and about three to five months later, my mother, my sisters, and I were on our way, although separately, because that's how my parents arranged it.

I remember thinking that we were going on some kind of vacation, but when we got to the hotel, my mother introduced my sister and me to an older lady who said that she was going to take us to be with our dad. My mother stayed behind. That is how I found myself with the woman who was a stranger to me, driving my sister and me in her car somewhere.

I remember a great fear coming over me. I was an eleven-year-old girl, going to a completely strange place with a complete stranger. This strange lady was preparing us three cups of juice and dissolving two pills in each one. I later learned that it was indeed Benadryl to knock us out. I started feeling very sleepy and closed my eyes. When I woke up, I was outside a McDonald's, and the strange lady had bought chicken nuggets and hamburgers for us. Then she took us to my grandmother's house in Austin. The next morning, my mother showed up with a man, to whom my grandmother gave some money. I remember looking through the window and seeing my mother, looking very scared, with a huge bruise on her forehead. As soon as she saw us, she burst out crying.

My father arrived later in the week in a car to pick us up, and we were on our way to Milwaukee. This really did feel like a vacation at first. Everything was as beautiful and white as snow. We were staying with my aunt, who had a beautiful home, and also owned a restaurant where my father started working. When it was time for us to move out of my aunt's house, my dad rented a small "apartment."

The whole apartment was the size of the room where my sister and I used to sleep back in Mexico. That's when I started realizing this wasn't the happy little vacation that I had initially thought it was. Starting school was the scariest of all, coming to a place where you can't understand the language and have to adapt to a new culture. It was all very overwhelming.

Beside all this, my oldest sister and I suffered domestic violence from my dad. He had always been my hero figure growing up. This completely destroyed me, and our relationship was never the same. We had no one to cry out to except some friends from school. Unfortunately, the only people who were there for us were all gang members. We didn't become gang members, but we were always around them.

Then, suddenly again, my dad decided to leave Milwaukee because of health issues, and we ended up back in Austin. I liked that idea because I would be closer to my mom's side of my family and felt more secure with them. I went to high school and, at the same time, took my cosmetology course. I was a good student, and a few days after my graduation, I received the best and worst news: I passed my exam to get my cosmetology license, and I was accepted to Texas State University. It was a dream come true!

My dad didn't even say how proud he was. All he said was that we couldn't afford education and not to waste my time studying and preparing for a job because I was undocumented. This broke my heart. It hurt that my dad said it and that his words were true. It didn't matter how smart I was or how good my grades were; I was not allowed to study or work and do what I wanted because of my immigration status.

So, I started working as a hairstylist, and that's where I met my husband, first becoming friends and then falling in love. My husband came to this country as an unaccompanied minor when he was a teen, and he has been working ever since to support his family and siblings in Mexico. We had three beautiful babies, and I was so happy to finally have the family I had always dreamed of. I had a wonderful, hard-working man who took three jobs to support not only our little family but his parents as well, who were still in Mexico.

We bought a small trailer home and found a spot to rent in Bastrop, Texas, until we could save enough money to buy our own land. We had big dreams to build our own home, to own it ourselves, and not to pay rent anymore.

Then, on December 17, 2019, came the worst day of my life. My husband was stopped by a sheriff's deputy just a couple of blocks away from our house. When he asked for my husband's driver's license, which he obviously didn't have (because undocumented immigrants are not allowed by Texas state law to apply for a driver's license), the deputy, at his own discretion, decided to detain him. So even though we need a driver's license to drive around everywhere, the law prevents us from doing so. Instead, many of us drive with the constant fear of being stopped by law enforcement officers.

My husband was detained and taken into immigration custody. He was transferred to Pearsall South Texas detention center on December 24, was there for six months, and then was deported. This shook me to the core. My world crumbled to pieces. My husband had provided me with all the happiness and stability that I had longed for, ever since it was so strangely taken away from me as a child that day in Mexico.

I had to reach out to people for help and have become part of an activist organization that has given me emotional support, empowered me, and helped me with fundraisers to provide for the immediate needs of my family. I work in a food trailer, struggling to make ends meet during a global pandemic and to pay the attorney's fees for trying to get my husband out of the detention center. I am a single mom now, taking care of everything for my three children, one of whom has special needs. It's very hard and lonely. I miss my husband so much.

I am terrified of the police and county deputies in Bastrop. There is a history of racism among them. They constantly follow and harass our community, looking for any excuse to detain us and for undocumented immigrants who can be deported. People don't even call the cops if they feel in danger because the fear of being taken away from their families is much worse than anything else.

I came to this country when I was eleven years old, fearfully sitting in the back seat of a stranger's car. Now I am twenty-nine years old, and while I am not that little girl anymore, I face that same fear every day when I get in my car. But now I am in the driver's seat, nervously looking in the rearview mirror where I can also see my precious children sitting in the back seat. I watch them, and I am fearful for me, for them, for what could happen. What if I get stopped just like my husband and taken away from my three children, my American children?

Immigrant families like mine are being separated and their lives destroyed over something as common as a driver's license. Like my parents in one way and completely unlike them in another, I want my children to be safe in the car. I don't want them to feel afraid like I did—like I do.

ELFEGA TORRES

"Ironically, I was so poor that I couldn't even afford to purchase the same food that we worked so hard to pick from the trees."

—ELFEGA TORRES

If I take a good look at my hands, there's my story right there. My hands have so much to say. What would I have done without them?

I was born in Mexico to a family of thirteen brothers and sisters. I was the one in the middle, and because my older siblings were male, I had to serve them while also caring for the younger ones. As a woman in Mexico, born in a *machista* family and context, that's how it is. As a woman, I had no voice, and I had no choice but to obey my father.

I used to love to study and go to school. I was very good at math; I even helped my dad do the numbers in his business. But at the young age of eleven years old, my parents pulled me out of school so that I could work in the house and help my dad with his business. My true desire was to continue studying in school. Even though I had to do so many home chores, I tried to finish them quickly just so that I could go to school. I had to wake up very early to do all this. I was just a child, but with this workload, I was stripped of my childhood.

When I turned fourteen years old, my parents wanted an arranged marriage for me. They practically wanted to sell me so that they could have more money. When I found out about this, I wanted to escape and planned to do so with the help of one of my dad's workers. He was thirty years old and helped me run away, but he tricked me and abused me sexually and psychologically for many years. I lived in constant terror. I had two children with him, who grew up hungry and malnourished. I became malnourished as well. When I finally got help from his sister to escape, I left him. I ran away with my one-year-old son and was pregnant with my daughter. I had nowhere to go, so I went from one house to another until I ended up at my parents' house again. Things only got worse there. When I arrived, my father wanted to hit me with a rope, but I told him that he couldn't do it because I was pregnant. Food security and money were an issue, so after my daughter was born, I started to work. I worked two jobs to provide for my kids and my mom, who was taking care of them while I was at work.

Then everything changed. The man who kidnapped and raped me came back, looking for me. He was following me and I didn't know that he was doing it. He even paid money to one of my youngest brothers to get my son out of the house. I had to stop everything that I was doing because I was terrified of him and of what he could do to us. So when my older brother arrived from California, I illegally crossed the border from Tijuana to California with him. I couldn't take my kids with me, and this grieved me, so I left them behind with my mother. But I didn't want to leave them with her for very long because I didn't want my kids to go through the same kind of abuse that I had gone through with my family. My plan was to save up enough money so that eventually, I could bring them with me.

This was my opportunity to escape, to leave all my traumatic experiences behind me. Inevitably, the trauma followed me and still haunts me to this very day. It even tries to prevent me from sharing my story like this.

When we got to the border of Tijuana, we tried to cross at nighttime but got caught by Border Patrol and put in jail. A few hours later, they bused us to the border of Tijuana. Back in Tijuana, we tried a second time, and we made it. I was seventeen years old when I set foot in California. My older sister was already there, and she helped me find a job as a nanny and maid for an American family. I lived and worked in their home, where I had to clean, cook, and nanny their three kids after school. The woman who hired me was a stay-at-home mom, and she was bored, so she taught me to play cards and drink beer with her. It was the first time that I'd had alcohol in my life.

I was only getting paid $50 for a full week of work without any breaks. I needed more money so that I could save to bring my children from Mexico, so I asked my older siblings if I could work with them in agriculture work. They told me it was hard work, and they were right. It was arduous work, but I still preferred it to working as a maid for that family.

I moved in with my siblings. The four of us rented out a garage in a home. We had no kitchen or bathroom, but at least the landlord allowed us to come inside her house and use them. That's how you do it when you're undocumented; you live crowded together in small spaces.

Every day, I woke up early in the morning between one and three o'clock to make breakfast and lunch, burritos and tacos. We had to drive to different farms and wait for work to start. Moreover, agricultural work is seasonal, and when it rains, there is no work. The workers in the fields were immigrant Latinos from Mexico, for the most part. It was very difficult work to do. I saw several farm workers suffer from heatstroke and dehydration, and they gave up. We had no benefits, no restroom, no cafeteria, no safety equipment, and not even a space to sit down in chairs for just a while.

The pay was also miserable. It was based on how much we collected, so if we wanted to earn more money, we had to work even harder. I started working as a picker of lemons and oranges. They paid me $12.50 for twelve orange bags and $14.50 for sixteen lemon bags. This was all handpicked oranges and lemons. The way you pick them is by getting up on a ladder and then picking them and putting them in bags. I also picked avocados and was paid $12 per box. Each box had several bags inside it.

Some farms had shorter trees, but others had trees that were very tall. We had to use a ladder up to eighteen feet high to pick the fruit. So every day was spent going up and down the ladder, sometimes falling down the ladder and getting seriously injured. Then we had to carry the heavy sacks of fruits on our shoulders. When a sack is full, it weighs around 40 pounds. We needed about sixteen sacks to fill the bin, which was around 3 × 3 feet wide and 3 feet high. We were paid $14.50 for each bin.

It was backbreaking and risky work. That's when my back problems began for me, and I still have them today. After work, we were all exhausted and would go to bed early, not only because we were exhausted, but also because we had to wake up very early the next day, and so on; it repeated day after day.

To me, the hardest thing was picking corn. The first time, I wore plastic gloves on my hands and wrapped them in bandages, but even like that, my hands bled every day. I had trouble feeding myself because I couldn't even hold a spoon with my hands; and it was like this every day, bleeding and hurting, but I had to use my hands the next day for work.

Considering how difficult and risky, and yet how essential this kind of work really is, it's so underpaid. In addition, there are people and companies that take advantage of immigrants. It happened to me and to many others: after we had worked packing oranges for a company for a whole week, they told us to leave without paying us and threatened us that if we didn't, they would call the police or immigration. Ironically, I was so poor that I couldn't even afford to purchase the same food that we worked so hard to pick from the trees. Unfortunately, this continues to be the same way today.

On top of it all, we faced another difficulty: the border patrol, better known as *la migra*, was always after us, trying to catch us and deport us. We lived in constant fear. I remember being fearful of the Pacific Bell vans because they had the same white and blue colors as *la migra*.

All we wanted to do was to work. We never engaged in any criminal activity or got in trouble with the police. Despite the arduous and risky work, I was not afraid of getting my job done. I was very afraid of the Border Patrol. While working with my brothers, we were deported to Tijuana about four times. I remember the Border Patrol agents taking away our food and eating it right in front of us, knowing that we were hungry, mocking us, and laughing at us, saying it was delicious. We suffered so much, not only from the US Border Patrol but also from the police in Tijuana, who would stop us, take us to an empty field, search us, and then steal all the money we had. It was very scary on both sides of the border.

Every time that I was deported, I would choose to cross the border again and come back because it was my only option to survive in this world. I found out about the packing jobs and decided to get a job packing green squash, corn, and later, avocado. It was difficult because I had to stand on my feet for long hours, but I learned to pack fast. In the warehouse, the job was easier, and they paid by the box. They paid about ten to fifteen cents per box, so I put a lot of effort into working quickly. I stocked up to five hundred boxes daily to earn more money. There were days that we had so many orders, and we had to work fourteen hours with no breaks and no food. At the end of my shift, I remember feeling dizzy and weak. Sometimes, I didn't even know where the building exit was. It was a difficult job, too, but at least I never saw the immigration patrol on my way to work. With so much to worry about, at least I didn't have to worry about that.

I worked for seven months so that I could save money to bring my children, even though it was very little money. Then with my kids here, I had to work even harder. Because agriculture is seasonal, I had to work different jobs. I worked mornings as a packer in the warehouse, and at night I worked a second job cleaning offices.

In 1987, I got a huge break. President Ronald Reagan declared amnesty for all the undocumented immigrants, and because I worked in agriculture, I qualified to become a citizen. Because my kids were part of my family unit, I was able to arrange to get citizenship status for them as well. This was such a relief for me and had such a huge impact on my life. I was so grateful to President Reagan that I named my third son Ronald after him.

No more deportations for me, or fear of the police or Border Patrol. That terrible fear that I had experienced for years was gone. But it is the same fear that immigrants still experience today.

Even though now I am now a US citizen and have an ID and rights, I feel compassion for all the undocumented immigrants who are living in this country, because I've been in the same situation that they're in now. I pray to God for them because they cross the border for the same reasons that I once did. They come escaping poverty or violence. They come seeking a better life for their children.

Becoming a US citizen allowed me to finally leave the packing job. After years of working two daily jobs, I applied for a job as a custodian at Nordstrom, working the night shift. I was 27 years old then, and while my children were in school, I started doing some of the things that I had wanted to do for a long time. I finally started taking English classes in the morning. "Learn the language," people say. When? I had been busy providing food and clean spaces for others. Then later, I attended community college to get an associate's degree.

From being a student, I went on to become an administrator, even though I had only completed the third grade. Finally, that eleven-year-old girl whose parents pulled her out of school so that she could help with domestic labor could finally quench her thirst and pursue the education that she had always longed for.

I still remember my scratchy, bleeding hands and the areas where the skin had peeled off. Those hands helped me grab apples, avocados, and corn in my farmworker days. They fed me and helped me rescue my kids. It seems like a long time ago, but farmworkers' conditions, unfortunately, haven't changed much since then.

Most pickers and packers are still undocumented, have no legal status, no health care, and no benefits. It's ironic because they are considered "essential" workers but still get paid very low wages. They're on the front lines of the pandemic, at even higher health risk, because they can't afford to stop working. They also still live together in small spaces, so if one gets sick, they're all going to get sick.

Today, I look at my hands and think, "What would I have done without them?" When I go to the grocery store, like everybody else, I simply reach out and grab an apple or an orange with my hands—no picking, no scratching, no thorns, no bleeding, no trembling, no pain, no packing. When I grab that apple with my hands, it feels so effortless, and I think, "How many things in life do we take for granted without knowing what's behind it?" and more important, "Who is behind this apple? Who is making it all possible and effortless for me and everybody else in the store?" Please think of these things, and remember my story, not just for my kids or me, but for all the immigrant farmworkers. Without them, we would have no food on our tables.

MARÍA ELENA
PARRA MARTINEZ

"I've learned that I cannot rely on only one source of income because I don't know what tomorrow may hold."

—MARÍA ELENA PARRA MARTINEZ

My mom would constantly tell me: "You can't stay here; you have to live a life that looks different than mine."

I was born on a farm in San Luis Potosí, México. My family worked in agriculture, and we did just fine. We had everything that we needed, and we didn't have financial problems. I was a "teacher for all ages"—the name they gave teachers who taught in rural areas, where there is only one teacher for all grades and levels. Not only was it hard work, but I had to walk many miles to get to the school. The bus would leave me at the town's station, and from there I had to walk alone between hills and mountains for more than 7 hours each way. So, I would walk between 12 and 14 hours a day. Sometimes I would do less time if I ran, and then it would take me about 4 hours each way. I got back into town around 10:00 or 11:00 p.m.

Looking back, I don't know how I managed to do that! I guess I was motivated to leave home, and teaching was my way to escape. More than just leaving home, my biggest motivation was that if I continued doing this work, I would be able to qualify for a scholarship to study at the university. My biggest dream was to become a lawyer.

Like many Mexican families, I lived in a home with domestic abuse, watching my mom suffer. I felt powerless and didn't know what to do, so I looked for a way to escape to the United States. I was twenty-three years old when I came to this country. I wasn't in real danger; I was just running from the violence that I saw at home.

I tried to apply legally for a visa and show paperwork that I had a good income, but they still denied my application. Throughout my life, I have seen how important it is to enter this country legally with a visa, because then you have a chance to continue applying to stay, but the problem is that visas are hard to come by, and many people are denied that opportunity. I was one of them.

I didn't know what else to do, so along with an acquaintance, we paid a "coyote" to help us cross the border. We rented a tiny office apartment where we lived with five other people. There were problems with that arrangement, so I moved to another apartment where I lived with eight men and two women, including myself. One of the men who lived there (who became my husband) protected and helped me, and got me a job working the night shift as part of a cleaning crew for H-E-B grocery stores.

We worked on several H-E-B locations (Waxahachie, Killen, Burnet, Luling, etc.). On our way to the different locations, we would be stopped by the sheriff and have to explain to him that we were on our way to work at the H-E-B store, and then he would let us go. We were driving at nighttime and at dawn in a crazy rhythm, every day without any holidays or rest days. H-E-B is always open except for two days a year. On one occasion, we fell asleep in the car and almost crashed into an eighteen-wheeler.

I earned $400 every two weeks, and my husband was paid $700 every two weeks. If I worked just a forty-hour week, that means I was paid $5 per hour, but I didn't work just 40-hour weeks. Worse, when our manager was on vacation, he only paid us half of our salary. He would come back and say that our work was not done well while he was gone. It was like we were paying him for his vacation and time off. These abuses of power and exploitation by people who have legal status against those of us who don't are seen over and over. Basically, our manager did whatever he wanted with us.

One day, I said, "I can't take this anymore, I can't continue working the night shift, and there is no future for me here." So I quit, and I found a job as a nanny. It turns out that I was more of a home manager than anything else. I was in charge of doing everything; cooking, taking care of the kids, driving them around, managing the bank deposits, cleaning the cars, etc. I really was in charge of practically everything.

I was paid $300 a week working from 7:00 a.m. to 7:00 p.m. every day, and sometimes I had to spend the night. It was too much stress. Aside from that, I was sexually harassed by the owner, the same abuse that I had been running from. With all the stress I was under, I ended up in the hospital. I filed a police report, and I got a restraining order against the abusers in that home. The police said that there are many reports like mine where employers abuse and exploit their employees.

Throughout my time living here in the United States, people have called me "wetback," "illegal," and even worse things. They have threatened to hit me, to deport me, and have tried to find ways to intimidate me, but I was never fearful until I worked in that home. I was completely traumatized, and it took me a long time to go back to work after the especially abusive situation with that family.

Time went by and returning to Mexico wasn't an option anymore. Long gone were the days where I could walk alone as I used to in Mexico; times had changed with a wave of terrible violence and organized crime. My in-laws had to escape because organized crime was threatening them and extorting them, asking them for a paid quota for their protection. That was the new reality of Mexico.

Also, the North American Free Trade Agreement (NAFTA) was initiated, and instead of helping the farmers in Mexico, it ruined anyone who couldn't compete against the big investors. For example, an American purchased one thousand acres in Mexico and farmed tomatoes and chili's in competition with my dad, who only had four acres. He completely crushed my dad's business and continued eliminating any competition. Farmers stopped working their own lands. Small stores went out of business. So, because of NAFTA, many farmers immigrated to the US, including my brothers and my dad.

I've learned that I cannot rely on only one source of income because I don't know what tomorrow may hold. For that reason, I'm always looking for other sources of income to manage my home. I have started three small businesses. Right now, I work for a Canadian company in their health department, and I also own a cleaning company where I work and employ 25–30 people. I am self-employed and pay my taxes, even though, as an undocumented immigrant, I can't apply for any of the benefits my taxes help pay for. I don't have insurance and have always paid upfront for any doctor's appointment. I made a payment agreement with the hospital back when my daughter cut her toe on glass, and the ER costs were $6,000.

I am a mother of four children, all American citizens. I could never leave them or neglect them. I have also been a mom to my two little brothers who came here. They only knew how to work construction, and what makes construction work so hard is that not only are they underpaid, but many times contractors leave without paying their employees at all. They simply leave and stop returning phone calls, and there is no way of finding them, no way to hold them accountable when they can threaten to turn you in first.

My brothers were always struggling to make ends meet and to pay rent, and sometimes even though they worked hard, they had no money (for reasons just explained). We took in my brothers while they looked for another job. They had their own families, and we were all living together—at one point, we were fifteen people (six adults and eleven children) in a trailer home with three bedrooms.

This frustrated me and caused family problems. We couldn't live in this situation any longer, so we finally parted ways. It broke my heart because they continued to struggle. They were conned, got into trouble, and were then arrested. They had no money to pay for lawyers, who were asking them for more than $20,000 in legal fees. The worst part was that they left their own children behind because they were both arrested. One of my sisters-in-law stayed with her seven children, and SAFE (Stop Abuse for Everyone) helped her to get a job and to move forward.

The four children of my other brother had nowhere to go, so of course, I chose to take them in. It wasn't something that I had to think through or analyze. My nieces and nephews have undergone severe trauma. I simply saw their need, that they had nowhere to go, and I took them in. Otherwise, social services would have taken them, and who knows what would have happened to them. I don't receive any government aid for any of them, even though they're all American citizens, like my own four children at home.

This has caused strains in my marriage, but I cannot leave these children. Is the solution to send them to my sister-in-law's family back in Mexico, where women in the family prostitute themselves to survive? It's just not an option. Besides, these children are American citizens and have the right to be in their own country. When their parents are freed from jail, then we can talk about what's next for them, but until then, they're staying with me.

Living in this country has been about survival. I didn't think I would live this way, but I wouldn't go back to the violence that reigns back in Mexico. Every challenge is preparing me and making me stronger. I know what my situation is, but I'm not intimidated. I always have a plan. In case I get deported, I also have a Plan B. I won't leave my kids behind, even when they're American citizens and have the right to be here, and my children know who they need to contact in case something happens to me.

In this country, I found God. I learned to fight for my rights as a woman and to be treated with respect. There are so many women who, like my mom, suffer domestic violence, and they have no one to turn to.

I have lived a different life, just as my mom wanted. She would have been proud. I want to leave a legacy my children can be proud of, too: a legacy of an immigrant woman, who after everything she went through, was able to be caring, serve God, and accomplish everything she wanted.

RAÚL GARCÍA

"I have tried to do everything the right way . . . twenty-five years later, and I still don't have a green card."

—RAÚL GARCÍA

We crossed the border from Mexico to Laredo when I was five years old. We were all in a van, my mom and four siblings, seeking to be reunited with my dad. For several years, he would come and go, working and sending us money. My parents decided it was time to all be together, and so we moved to Texas.

Our family was reunited, but we were living as undocumented immigrants, and that presented challenges for my parents. My mom was worried about our future and very concerned about the possibility of us getting separated because of our immigration status. So she was constantly seeking legal help.

I started to hear about legal paperwork and hiring lawyers when I was about seven years old. I remember how desperate and concerned my mother was to get us a lawyer to try to solve our legal status. I heard her talk about it constantly, but I didn't really understand any of it until I got older.

I remember when she finally hired an immigration lawyer recommended by someone. Her name was Yolanda, and my mom paid her hundreds of dollars from her life savings. It was money she had saved working her two restaurant jobs. Yolanda's fees were expensive, but my parents worked out a payment plan with her so that they would pay her legal fees monthly. They also provided her with all the legal documents that she requested, including our birth certificates. All our hopes were on her, and she promised to help us.

It turned out that after completing all the payments, suddenly Yolanda wouldn't answer our phone calls. She completely disappeared. Desperate and upset, my mom continued looking for this woman and finally met someone who had also been swindled with broken promises of getting legal status. It seems that this would be a pattern in our lives for years to come: a lot of empty promises, fraud, and exploitation, including by attorneys who simply took advantage of our situation and pocketed our money while doing nothing for our status.

That would be a terrible blow for anyone to endure, but my mother was relentless. She continued to look for ways to get a green card for all of us and hired another lawyer, but that didn't work out either. Through all of this, I have learned that the immigration system is very complicated, that there is a lot of purposeful misinformation and inaccurate information about how to get legal status in America, due in part to the constant changes in immigration rules and procedures, and there aren't many people who know and understand how the system really works, including the immigration lawyers!

When I was younger, I didn't realize how important having papers and legal documents really was. For so long, I thought of myself as just a regular neighborhood kid. I didn't realize I had to worry about getting deported. Then, like most teens, I didn't know those poor choices made as a young man could impact the future of getting a green card later in life. Those same choices don't affect other teens' ability to live here. These are things no one teaches you in school, things you aren't even remotely aware of when you're living your everyday life.

In my early twenties, I was reckless and was caught with marijuana and driving under the influence. This is a mistake one makes when young, something that can happen to anybody, the kind of thing that has happened to people we all know. But for me, an undocumented immigrant, the consequences of that mistake have impeded my being able to obtain the precious green card that would allow me to become a legal resident.

I started working at the age of thirteen to help my family pay bills. When I was seventeen, I had to file for a permit to work at a company. I have been using a work permit since then to legally work, reapplying, and making application payments every two years for that permit. I've been doing this for twenty-five years now.

At the time of my DUI, my parents were still taking care of my permit paperwork, and I didn't realize how these infractions could put me at risk for not getting a green card, and worse, of potentially being deported and separated from my family, and losing everything I'd worked so hard to achieve.

As an undocumented immigrant, any mistake you make, no matter how small or how long ago it happened, the consequences are harsh as well as costly, and I don't only mean financially. Any little mistake can cost you your life.

At the age of twenty-two, I started my own business, tiling and remodeling homes and businesses. I was always taken by architecture, and I developed a gift for building things. This gave me a clearer purpose and vision for my life. It was then that I thought I should work towards getting my green card so that I didn't have to renew my work permit every two years and so that I didn't have to constantly be worried about my legal status. I would feel free to fulfill my dreams.

I hired a lawyer in San Antonio named Cristina. Like most lawyers, she told me everything would be fine, and I'd be successful at getting a green card, but all through the process, there were tons of issues. She lost my paperwork, miscommunicated things, told me contradictory things, and worked with an inexperienced staff of interns. I always felt like I was getting the run-around. Even though she knew I had a record, she insisted I was going to be fine. On the day of my green card interview, I showed up thirty minutes early, and Cristina showed up fifteen minutes late with an intern. The US Citizenship and Immigration Services (USCIS) officer said she did not want the intern in the room, and my lawyer proceeded to argue with the officer to convince her. She also forgot important paperwork for my case in her car. She was disorganized and unprofessional, and in the end, I was denied a green card. This stressful process took over three years and about $8,000, not including USCIS fees and lost work time.

After Cristina, I hired another lawyer, Mr. Wiztel, to help expunge my record. He was recommended to me by another attorney. I paid him $10,000, and he assured me that dismissal of my record would be good enough for immigration. Like most people, I did not know the difference between dismissal and expungement, but I trusted that a lawyer would. I later learned that dismissal is not good enough for immigration. He told me this was all he could do for me.

I grew increasingly worried that I might be deported after I was denied a green card, so I went and interviewed about a dozen lawyers, determined to find one who would actually help me. I chose Mr. Diaz because he was both a criminal and immigration lawyer. He basically told me he would help me clear my criminal record first through properly expunging my record. It took two years, but he did successfully expunge my record. He's working on resubmitting for another try at my green card. Two and a half years later, I have paid him about $15,000 and still don't have a green card or any clear idea of when that might happen. When I ask what's next or when I might expect progress, I'm never given any specifics, just vague answers about his thoughts of how to write up my case.

I'm grateful to God that I have a good job and am able to support myself and pay for lawyers. Unfortunately, my story has been one filled with empty promises that have cost me thousands of dollars. And this is not just my story, but the story of millions of undocumented immigrants who are seeking a path to citizenship, seeking to do it the right way, yet they are paying excessive legal fees to lawyers only to get taken advantage of over and over again.

I have tried to do everything the right way. I've been through all the necessary steps: I've hired professional help, including several attorneys who are supposedly equipped to help me with the process; spent thousands of dollars—almost $30,000 to be exact; and have reapplied for my work permit every two years. I've worked hard and stayed out of trouble since the unfortunate incident in my earlier years, yet here I am twenty-five years later, and I still don't have a green card.

It hasn't been easy. I've been working and paying taxes, although I don't get the benefits that citizens have. I am a hard worker who contributes to the economy of this country. I've had to save a lot of money to pay for each of these lawyers while running my business and helping to care for my parents and siblings.

I constantly worry about what my future may look like if I don't obtain a green card, especially with the broken immigration system and the laws constantly changing for the worse, without a clear path to citizenship. I understand the anxiety that my mom felt from the very beginning because it's the same anxiety that I've been living with since I became aware of my legal status and the uncertainty that overshadows my life.

JEAN CARLO VENCES

———————

"A simple mistake was made, and it changed the trajectory of our lives."

—JEAN CARLO VENCES

When I was little, about three years old, we went to visit family back in Mexico. When we returned to the US border, they wouldn't allow my mom back in the country. I don't even remember what the problem was; I just know we ended up having to stay in Mexico. A simple mistake was made, and it changed the trajectory of our lives.

Unlike many of my immigrant friends and family members, I had the fortune of being born in the United States; but my mom's status, or lack of status, limited my own. As a child, I could do nothing, so that's how I ended up spending most of my life in Mexico.

My mom is a hard worker, always the first one up, and she raised my two siblings and me on her own. She never went to college, so there are limited options for what she could do back in Mexico. As soon as I turned twenty-one, since I had the gift of citizenship, I was able to start the process to sponsor and petition for my mom's residence (green card). It's a process that normally takes at least a few years, sometimes many more, but for her, it miraculously took only one year. We couldn't believe it. With legal status in the US, my mom had more opportunities, and better opportunities opened up to her for work. My mom has taught me to work with excellence in everything that I do.

Most of my coworkers in the restaurants where I have worked are immigrants, and they don't have the gift of legal status, much less citizenship as I do, so they always joke with me about how I have it so easy. I can go in and out of the country and visit Mexico while they're living in fear of being deported and can't visit their families in Mexico. If they travel out of the country, like my mom did when I was little, they also risk not being allowed back in.

This hurts me, and it also makes me admire them for their hard work despite the daily risk that they take and the ongoing separation from family and their roots. If I could help them, I would. I hope that sharing my story may help them.

Look into the kitchen of any restaurant that you go to and see who's working behind the scenes washing your dishes and cooking your food. No matter what type of food it is—Indian, Asian, Mediterranean, fusion—it's the same thing. I've worked everywhere from P. Terry's to the Dobie Tower and Levy, where I am now, and there are always Latinos in the kitchen, working very hard.

I'm proud of my roots, and I should not have to change or give up parts of myself for anybody. I'm not ashamed of who I am, but my coworker thinks that if you want to succeed in this country, you must get rid of your roots. We always argue about this. He is very focused on mastering the English language and being able to speak without an accent. He's also a white Latino, even though he is from Sinaloa, Mexico. So many people don't even think that he is from Mexico. On the other hand, I have brown skin and an accent, and I am the one who is a US citizen, but having status doesn't change anything for me. I am treated as if I am an undocumented immigrant.

People automatically assume that because I work in the kitchen and speak Spanish, I don't speak or understand English. I have been asked by a manager, who is white, not to speak Spanish at work. It feels like I'm always being limited to one language; by some, I'm believed to be incapable of more and by others I'm told not to use all of my abilities. At another job, when they were looking for a new manager, and I was the obvious choice, they overlooked me because of my accent and the fact that my English was slower. I work so hard, but it's not enough. It's plain racism. Those kinds of assumptions are based on prejudices; and it bothers me that there are a lot of assumptions and prejudices about language, about immigrants, about what we are capable of.

I have had several instances in which white people assumed that if I was speaking in Spanish with someone else, we must be talking about them. I always reply that if I have something to say about someone, I'll say it to his or her face. But when people feel uncomfortable because they don't know Spanish, it seems that I am the one they try to shame. I love Spanish, my native tongue, my first language, and I am not ashamed of who I am, of my background, or of my culture. If it bothers people enough, it should be motivation to learn Spanish, not to assume things about me. Speaking two languages is better than speaking one; I know from experience.

We live in a multicultural country where there is a lot of diversity, with many countries and cultures represented. It is a country made of immigrants, and the only ones who are locals are the Native Americans. It amazes me that most people are not able to understand this or accept this, and I think it's probably because white nationalism is so ingrained in this country. If my talent, my roots, or the fact that I speak Spanish offends people, that is not my problem. Are you proud of who you are? I am.

At the beginning of the pandemic, I searched everywhere and couldn't find a single job. Those first three months were hard because we were all in a panic, and I was worried because my life savings were dwindling. But then things started to get better, and opportunities opened up for me to work in the restaurant business. I've always wanted to learn how to cook, so this has been a great opportunity for me. Now cooks are in high demand—people still want to be fed. But working in the kitchen is hard, and the hours are long.

In my job at the Dobie Tower, I was doing thirteen-hour shifts. I had to open for breakfast, do catering, then clean the kitchen without breaks or eating anything. The manager wasn't even helping us in the kitchen with everything we had to do. My restaurant jobs have made it clear that people don't respect Latinos as human beings. Because of their assumptions, people dehumanize immigrants and Latinos in the kitchen. For example, in that job at Dobie, I wouldn't be left alone working because they were afraid that I was going to steal something.

What people don't realize is that for a Latino immigrant, to steal would risk everything. Latino immigrants have so much more to lose if caught. A simple infraction or a minor transgression can get us in jail and then deported, so it's unlikely that we will commit a crime. I'm not saying that we're perfect; nobody is perfect, but we have a lot more to lose than anyone else.

If something went missing, I would be the one to blame automatically, not the white workers. What's ironic about this is that it was the white kids who were doing the stealing at that job. They would let the white kids stay behind alone, but when money started missing, nobody would suspect them. It got so bad, but they still never looked at the white kids, even though it was obvious. Instead, it was decided that no one would stay, that we all had to leave at the same time.

Now I am working in a company called Levy, and it's been a challenge because there's a lot of pressure. I have high standards and try to make quality food, but it's a fast pace, so it's like I'm being asked to sacrifice quality for speed. In addition, we constantly get young white temps and volunteers who don't know how to do this work and don't know how to interact with us in the kitchen. I recently discovered that some of the folks who volunteer come from an organization called Justice for Our Neighbors, which helps immigrants with their legal work. That motivated me, knowing that a good part of the profits from the food that I cook will be shared with this organization that directly helps immigrants and educates people to correct misinformation about immigrants and the immigration legal process.

I have another motivation: the company that I am working for manages a food business in New York as well, and that's where I am headed with my music. If I keep working here, then I'll ask to move there.

There's more to me than meets the eye, more to me than all the assumptions people make. People see me (or don't see me) working in the kitchen, but they don't know this work is my means to another end. They don't look at me and see I am a musician. Music is my passion. This is who I am.

I have studied guitar and flute. Back in Mexico, I was a recognized musician; I had a jazz band and a flamenco jazz duet. I earned a living playing music. I left Mexico and decided to come to the US because I was starting to catch the attention of organized crime with my music. Several friends of mine have been kidnapped or have been victims of the cartels. In Guanajuato, where I lived, there is the Cartel de Santa Rosa de Lima, and it's growing. There is a power struggle between cartels. This has made it very dangerous, and I was afraid to go out and play my music.

Here, I have continued to pursue my musical ambitions. I am part of a reggae Latino band called Roleros Cosmicos. I don't want to stay in the same place. I want to keep growing and going up the ladder. That's why I'm here now. My career in the kitchen is a way to achieve my goals with my music, one of which is to eventually move to New York and take my music to another level. In the meantime, I will keep working hard, holding my head high, and taking advantage of every opportunity that life provides me.

"The shortest distance between truth and a human being is a story."

—ANTHONY DE MELLO

PART II

The Truth in Our Stories

IMMIGRANTS CONTRIBUTE

From taxes to building infrastructure to creating jobs, immigrants contribute to the US economy, in great contrast to the tired, adverse, unsubstantiated claims meant to scapegoat and create fear. For context, the foreign-born population in the United States peaked in 1890 at 14.8 percent (this includes both undocumented individuals and those with legal status). Currently, the undocumented immigrant population makes up less than 4 percent of the total population living in the United States. This may be surprising, considering how often words like "crisis" and "surge" are used in relation to immigration news and conversation. The National Academies of Sciences, Engineering, and Medicine released a report in 2017[29] that concludes that "immigration has an overall positive impact on long-run economic growth in the U.S." and that any impact on native-born workers' wages and employment is minimal.

In 2019, the foreign-born population of the United States paid more than $492 billion in taxes, with more than half of all undocumented immigrants using an Individual Tax Identification Number (ITIN) to file tax returns. Even those immigrants who do not file tax returns pay sales tax and applicable property tax. If all eleven million undocumented immigrants currently residing in the United States were granted citizenship, the Institute on Taxation and Economic Policy estimates tax contributions would grow by $2.1 billion per year. New American Economy (NAE), a bipartisan research organization, estimates the spending power of immigrants in 2019 totaled $1.3 trillion.[30]

Immigrants contribute to the economy through job creation, too. NAE reports over 3.2 million immigrant entrepreneurs in the United States, including several of our storytellers. In a comprehensive study by Ben Jones of the Kellogg School of Management at Northwestern University and his colleagues,[31] data indicate that immigrants create more jobs than they take. Whether a small, medium, or large business, immigrants create new businesses at higher rates than does the US-born population. Additionally, immigrant entrepreneurs pay higher wages and tend to be more inventive, holding more patents than businesses founded by US-born entrepreneurs. In our stories, Sandra and her husband exhibit their creativity and inventiveness as successful investors, flipping homes they purchase and remodel (and employing workers for these projects).

"People who are willing to pick up and move to another country—into the unknown—are risk-takers. And there are empirical studies that indicate this," says Jones. "They are going to be masters of their own destiny. And that is a personality trait of entrepreneurs."[32] In our stories, Patricia shares about running her husband's welding company and starting her own business. María Elena runs three businesses! Raúl started his construction and remodeling business at twenty-two years old.

In fact, immigrants make up 24.8 percent of the construction workforce in the United States, including Ángel, who learned every part of how to build a house from the foundation. Immigrants work in several other critical roles in building up US infrastructure. The Center for Migration Studies released a report in May 2020[33] breaking down data about immigrant workers in various categories of essential critical infrastructure (as defined by the US Department of Homeland Security). The report's data show the foreign-born population makes up over 30 percent of hotel workers, 22 percent of transportation workers, over 20 percent of essential manufacturing workers, and over 21 percent of warehouse, distribution, and fulfillment workers.

Immigrants are not limited to contributing to economic growth; we grow as a culture through the contributions of immigrant artists, musicians, authors, and entertainers. Jesús and Jean Carlo share their creative gifts, joining with countless others to enrich our cultural imagination, shape emotional expression, and strengthen our capacity for reflection and wonder.

IMMIGRANTS PROVIDE

Elfega says her story is in her hands: her hands, Patricia's family's hands, Sandra's and her family's hands—they are the hands that feed us. Despite a history of relying on immigrants for the food on our tables, including 246 years of enslaved laborers, immigrant farmworkers continue to face harsh demands and field conditions, wage theft and exploitation, and most recently, the risk of coronavirus and COVID-19, as food cannot be picked remotely.

Imagine, like Sandra, you are at the grocery store picking out a cucumber. You check the size and condition of the product, but do you think of whose hands helped get that cucumber from the soil to the store? Do you think about how many cucumbers the farmworkers' hands picked the day they picked your particular selection? Do you think about how much the farmworkers were paid for the day's labor as you check the price?

The low farmworker wages and few work condition regulations existing at state and federal levels often lack actual enforcement. In 2008, the Centers for Disease Control reported that farmworkers are twenty times more likely to die of heat stress than any other category of worker in the United States.[34] Since then, temperatures have only increased due to climate change. The State of Washington enacted emergency heat rules in July of 2021 for temperatures over 100 degrees, requiring employers to provide shade and paid cooling breaks. But enforcement relies on individuals to report violations, which means workers or activists bear the burden, the former at the risk of retaliation from their employers.

Temperatures get hot in the kitchen, too, where immigrants are washing dishes and working as cooks to put food on the tables outside our homes. It is a role Tony loves to play, though the pandemic has cut him off from it. As Jean Carlo said, it does not matter the type of cuisine; immigrants are in the kitchen, making up over 20 percent of all restaurant employees. Additionally, between the fields and the table, immigrants make up over 26 percent of food and beverage processing workers.

Besides nourishing our bodies with food, immigrants play a critical role at all levels of health care. If it was not personally prioritized before, the pandemic prompted the nation to pay careful attention to cleaning and sanitation practices. Like María Elena, keeping our grocery stores clean and now employing 25 individuals in the cleaning company she started, immigrants make up 28 percent of building cleaners and janitors. In the hospitals where some of those workers clean, 16 percent of all the workers are immigrants. But hospitals aren't the only place we receive care; residential health care facilities rely on immigrants for 17 percent of their workers, and more than one in four home health workers and aides to the elderly are immigrants. Immigrants make up 24 percent of the workers manufacturing medical equipment and instruments used by health care workers. At the same time, research work and laboratories running tests and reporting results depend on immigrants for one out of every five workers. And the medicine you take? Immigrants make up one in four workers in pharmaceutical manufacturing.

Imagine if all these construction, hotel, restaurant, manufacturing, janitorial, and health workers simply left their jobs. Patricia mentioned participating in the "Day Without Immigrants" in 2017, a combination protest, boycott, and strike where some immigrants stayed home from school and work while some businesses completely closed for the day to show support for their employees. The protest was like an ironic taste of what was being threatened by the president: the deportation of all undocumented immigrants. Of course, not all immigrants could join the protest, as employers threatened termination for anyone who did not show up for work. The rhetoric in recent years has not just threatened deportation of all 11.4 undocumented immigrants already integrated into our communities, but it escalates the threat to the entire foreign-born community, with calls to denaturalize or strip citizenship away.

Alongside all the numbers already given, remember one more: the foreign-born population, both undocumented individuals and those with legal status, comprise only 14.4 percent of the total population in the United States. That means they fill essential critical infrastructure roles at a disproportionate rate, higher than their native-born counterparts do. If anti-immigrant propagandists and nativists got their way not just for a day but for good, who would provide for us then?

IMMIGRANTS DESERVE DIGNITY AND JUSTICE

As Jean Carlo stated, undocumented immigrants are not perfect, but they have more to risk if they break the law. Raúl is still suffering the consequences of a DUI in his youth, now preventing him from moving forward in his pursuit of legal status. Yet, Donald Trump went from being a joke candidate for political pundits reporting on the primaries to the Republican nominee for president by making the foundation of his platform the old lie that immigrants are criminals. Report after report after report (do a web search!) rejects that platform and presents the extension of Jean

Carlo's statement: immigrants are less likely than US citizen counterparts to commit crimes.

Yet, the budget for the US Border Patrol is eighteen times what it was in 1990. The $8.3 billion budget for Immigration and Customs Enforcement has almost tripled since 2003, giving immense power to a law enforcement agency dedicated to terrorizing less than 4 percent of the US population and their US citizen family members. For comparison, the 2020 budget request for the Federal Bureau of Investigation (FBI), the federal law enforcement agency responsible for protecting the entire population of the nation from terrorism, espionage, cyberattacks, major white-collar crimes, and significant violent crimes, totaled $9.3 billion.

Members of Austin Region Justice for Our Neighbors attended the House State Affairs Committee hearing of the Texas Legislature in the spring of 2019, listening to testimony after testimony pleading for support for HB 35, created to give access to a driver's permit for those without a social security number. One committee member implied that he was sympathetic with the hardships being shared but that his obligation was to his citizen constituents. Of course, his statement ignores the fact that many of his citizen constituents are children who are too young to advocate for themselves and rely, as a result, on their noncitizen parents to provide for them. But in doing so, these parents risk what Ángel and Miriam's husband faced for being caught without a driver's license: imprisonment and deportation.

For US citizens caught driving in the state of Texas without a license, the first offense can carry a fine of up to $200 (though no minimum penalty is required); if a second conviction occurs within a year of the first conviction, the required punishment is a fine of not less than $25 or more than $200. If a third conviction occurs within the year, confinement in the county jail becomes a real possibility.

The 14th Amendment states: "No State shall make or enforce any law which shall abridge the privileges or immunities of citizens of the United States; nor shall any State deprive any person of life, liberty, or property, without due process of law;

nor deny to any person within its jurisdiction the equal protection of the laws." The amendment starts with discussing protections for citizens but note that it shifts to any person's use as it outlines the right to life, liberty, and property and equal protection of the law. Does getting pulled over for tinted windows that just passed inspection, resulting in six months of imprisonment and deportation/separation from family, sound equal to a possible but not required fine of $200?

While the government is willing to collect taxes from undocumented immigrants (to great gain, as has already been described), these same contributors do not have access to the full public benefits that their taxes fund. The next time you hear someone say that undocumented immigrants are a drain, pulling public benefits away from taxpayers, remember Adrián's mother and the payment plan María Elena arranged to pay for hospital bills for her daughter. Not only are undocumented immigrants unable to access medical assistance benefits (funded in part by their taxes), but they cannot even buy insurance (including through the Affordable Care Act). Even when individuals are granted the legal status of asylum, access to certain public benefits is only available for the first 6–8 months.

It's not just immigrants who bear the physical, mental, and emotional trauma of inhumane policies and unthinkable choices; US citizen children of immigrants have their unalienable rights discounted, forcing the trauma of separation, which Carmen's children faced, and which Patricia's children feared they would meet again. The alternative to separation is to go with their parents to a country they do not know and where they are not citizens, which means forcing children to give up access to critical medical care, educational and work opportunities, and face growing violence. Shouldn't it bother us all that any US citizen, especially children, can be told to choose between giving up their family or their natural rights and freedoms?

Undocumented immigrants, as you have heard in their own stories, want to pursue legal status in the United States. The problem is not a willfulness to circumvent the law, but the convoluted, lengthy, and expensive process we currently call the legal path to lawful permanent residency and citizenship in the United States. As if the government's fees for applications were not expensive enough (for example, the application fee to register for permanent residence ranges from $75 to $1440, not including expenses for required medical exams), it is near impossible to navigate through the legal process without the assistance of an attorney. Legal representation costs thousands of dollars for those lucky enough to secure it, even for "simple" applications such as the Deferred Action for Childhood Arrivals (DACA). Of course, we know from Raúl that there are attorneys (as well as people imitating attorneys) who will take money without moving the case forward, or charge exorbitant amounts like the legal fees María Elena's brothers accumulated. Carmen spent thousands and thousands on appeals processes. And to think, immigrants weren't even required to have visas before 1924.

Even if you successfully file your application for Lawful Permanent Resident, the current wait time for spouses, siblings, and unmarried children of green card carriers is anywhere from 2–22 years. If you look at sibling-sponsored applications, the wait jumps to a range of 14–24 years. You may remember Jean Carlo's shock at how quickly his mother received her green card. Meanwhile, Patricia has been waiting for over 20 years.

Contrary to popular belief, television shows, and movies, a marriage certificate isn't a magic loophole to legal status. In fact, many undocumented immigrants face abuse and threats from US citizen spouses (and other partners, for that matter) who use their lack of status as a weapon and a way to maintain abusive control. This is in addition to employers' abuse and exploitation, which we heard in the stories of farmworkers and María Elena's brothers working in the construction industry. Withholding wages, ignoring overtime, unreasonably long shifts, and rigorous demands are all too common. Yet, these types of crimes go primarily unprosecuted because of fear of contacting and engaging with any type of law enforcement agency. So not only are immigrants less likely to commit a crime, but they are also afraid to seek justice for the crimes committed against them.

While the stories shared in this book are full of hardship and shadows, the immigrants who share these stories shine with resilience and fortitude. These are just twelve stories; there are so many more around you and connected to you. Immigrants also provide for their families and extended families as María Elena does, opening paths for their children and the broader community to thrive through civic and religious engagement. Immigrants succeed and lead as employers, and before that as successful students, like Jesús and Adrián. Immigrants enrich our lives with art and music, like Jean Carlo and Jesús, and through activism and advocacy, like Carmen, fighting to advance justice for all.

CONCLUSION: THE CHALLENGE

Immigrant rights, and by extension the rights of all of us, are at stake. Donald Trump's ascension to the White House magnified the nation's fight over this issue, and his administration's actions only increased the hostility. In September of 2016, for example, the country witnessed massive walkouts on the part of Latino students who were protesting the Trump administration's removal of the DACA program, which grants protection from deportation for certain undocumented immigrants who were brought to the US as children. The Obama Administration initially established this program in 2012 as a response to congressional inaction on the development of comprehensive immigration reform. Because Congress refused to develop a sound plan regarding one of the most pressing issues in American politics, President Obama exercised his executive powers and launched DACA. It should be noted that DACA was also implemented after nearly a decade of massive grassroots organizing and direct action by undocumented youth across the country, who also demanded to the Obama administration that something had to be done. However, throughout his campaign, then-candidate Donald Trump criticized DACA, arguing that it allowed for the circumvention of current immigration laws, and once in the White House, he ended it.[35] DACA's termination unleashed a wave of protests by activists of all types who saw it as punitive, mean-spirited, and contrary to the ideals of what it means to be an American. Since then, it has remained hung up in Congress. To great relief for DACA recipients, however, the Supreme Court, in June 2020, eventually ruled that the Trump administration could not end the program.[36] Since then, unfortunately, states have increased their efforts to circumvent the court's ruling. For example, in Texas in July 2021 a federal court challenged the legality of DACA, arguing that it was an unlawful policy, and issued a moratorium on all new DACA applications.[37]

The fight for immigrant rights is held in other areas as well. Detention centers, for example, are a significant source of angst among activists because of the inhumane conditions that characterize them. In some places, immigrants are imprisoned outdoors. For instance, in South Texas, the Border Patrol holds immigrants in a pen-like detention center under a highway, where they remain exposed to the elements like scorching heat. Despite the protests about detention centers, including private prisons, they remain filled with immigrants who are often subjected to physical beatings, sexually molested or assaulted, and treated so hideously that some even commit suicide. In New Mexico, two immigrants attempted suicide in a detention center by slitting their wrists, and nineteen others have threatened to do the same.[38] In some instances, immigrants are tortured psychologically. Detained children, for example, are often asked to pick from which parent they want to be separated, or they are placed in cages. Especially troubling is the high number of immigrant deaths while under custody. According to the American Civil Liberties Union of Texas, 177 immigrants have died while under detention.[39] While excessive, the number of known deaths is the tip of the iceberg, as fatal encounters are believed to be even higher. Subsequently, activists have been calling for the abolition of immigrant detention centers, including private prisons. As complaints of abuse and inhumane, criminal, and discriminatory practices grow, activists remain hard-pressed to ensure their abolition.

Indeed, another source of anguish for immigrants is the Immigration and Customs Enforcement, or ICE, as it is commonly known. Since their formation, ICE agents have systematically and frequently arrested countless people without following due process, separating them from their families with little to no explanation. And the arrests never stop; according to their reporting in the first year of Donald Trump's presidency, ICE agents arrested more than 110,000 people, a 42 percent increase from the year before.[40] Additionally, ICE is also on record for deleting surveillance footage of immigrants who have died in their custody, evidence that was crucial in a pending wrongful death lawsuit. It also established plans to collect DNA from immigrants without their authorization. More recently, ICE moved hundreds of women who had severe medical conditions and failed to inform their lawyers and the public of their whereabouts. Especially heinous was ICE's family separation policy, which ripped thousands of children from their parents. This agency has acted outside the law for years with little oversight and no signs of slowing down. That Congress has allowed it to continue to operate as a covert law enforcement agency speaks volumes about how our society criminalizes immigrants and tolerates state-sanctioned terror against them.

Anti-immigrant sentiment and xenophobia have also altered our policy regarding asylum seekers. Under the Trump administration, the federal government proposed an unprecedented series of new fees for asylum seekers and immigrants hoping to stay in the US. Under the proposals, a new $50 fee would be imposed on asylum applications, while citizenship applications were priced at $595.[41] Additionally, the Trump administration considered restricting asylum seekers from working while living in the United States. Accordingly, they had to live in the country before applying for work permits for at least one year. It also directed ICE to start issuing fines to asylum seekers looking for sanctuary in churches, and rolled out its rapid asylum review and deportation processes; a pilot program aimed at carrying out the entire asylum process with immigrants behind bars, allowing only one day to contact a lawyer or family members. For those wishing to enter the country seeking asylum, the Migrant Protection Protocol (MPP) policy made that nearly impossible, no matter the terror they were escaping. Under this policy, those seeking asylum were forced to wait in Mexico for months on end, living in unsafe, hazardous conditions while their cases remained in limbo in US immigration courts.[42] With Joe Biden assuming the presidency in 2020, activists were confident that he would terminate the MPP policy, but that has not happened, and asylum seekers waiting in Mexico continue to endure severe forms of trauma.

Immigrant xenophobia has shattered the promise of citizenship for countless undocumented veterans who, despite their service in ensuring the safety and security of the US, found themselves banished from the country. Here again, activists believed that this policy would end once Biden took office, but it too remains, and the practice of blocking a pathway for citizenship for immigrant troops continues business as usual.

The xenophobia has also translated into violence; across the country, immigrants have found themselves physically assaulted. The most tragic example of this violence occurred in 2019 when white supremacist Patrick Crusius murdered twenty-two persons and injured another twenty-six others, mostly Mexicans, in the El Paso shooting. Emboldened by the anti-immigrant rhetoric peddled by his political leaders, Crusius drove over eleven hours to a border town to kill illegal immigrants.[43]

Although Trump is no longer in office, it seems that the Trump-era policies unfortunately continue to characterize the immigrant experience. With the pandemic in full swing, immigrants continue to be scapegoated by politicians, particularly by those who have done little to halt the spread of COVID-19. In March of

2020, for example, the government, under the guise of stopping the spread of COVID, upheld Title 42, which resulted in the mass expulsion of asylum seekers, since it was believed that they brought the coronavirus into the US, despite the arguments made by public health officials that immigrants do not spread the virus more than other groups throughout the US. Rather than blame the continuing pandemic on the low vaccination rate, politicians continue to hold immigrants responsible for the rising number of COVID cases.[11]

The reaction to all this nativism, xenophobia, and anti-immigrant sentiment has been massive resistance from activists who remain determined to place a moratorium on deportations, end ICE raids, abolish the Border Patrol, halt construction of a border wall, stop family separation, and close for-profit detention centers. A part of this resistance is medical professionals who denounced the conditions inside ICE facilities. The courts also have taken similar steps. For example, in a groundbreaking fifty-page opinion, a US district judge ordered the federal government to provide mental health screenings and other forms of treatment to thousands of immigrants traumatized by the family separation policy.[45] Another judge blocked a policy requiring immigrants to prove they have insurance or the financial resources for medical costs to obtain a visa. Yet another blocked the Public Charge Rule, a plan threatening to remove the legal status of immigrants eligible for programs like SNAP, Medicaid, and housing assistance.[46] Helping to lead the charge against racist, anti-immigrant legislation and policies include countless civil rights groups such as the Texas Organizing Project (TOP); the American Civil Liberties Union (ACLU); the Southern Poverty Law Center (SPLC); FIEL, a Houston-based nonprofit organization that helps young undocumented people; and United We Dream, an organization that connects undocumented youth with resources, to name a few.

Yet, there is much more work to be done. A great starting point in that endeavor is finding, documenting, preserving, and promoting the testimonies of immigrants.

It will be to our collective benefit to turn to and rely on the power of immigrant storytelling for several reasons. First, these experiences are worth telling. Second, they help us fully understand the immigrant experience. Third, they can redefine the distorted narrative that has come to frame immigration. The preceding pages, for example, illustrated how immigrants pay taxes, open businesses, improve the economy, harvest our foods, and build infrastructure, proving that they are essential and not deportable. Lastly, these experiences can contribute to the immigrant rights movement in significant ways, as they have the potential to change hearts and minds and ultimately affect policy. The other lesson to be learned is that we should all listen to the voices of immigrants in our communities; the truth is right here in their stories.

NOTES

INTRODUCTION

1. Arnold De Leon and Richard Griswold del Castillo, *North to Aztlan: A History of Mexican Americans in the United States*, 2nd ed., Harlan Davidson, Inc., 2006, p. 41.
2. Gabriela Gonzalez, *Redeeming La Raza: Transborder Modernity, Race, Respectability, and Right*, New York: Oxford University Press, 2018, pp. 62–65.
3. Arnold De Leon and Richard Griswold del Castillo, *North to Aztlan: A History of Mexican Americans in the United States*, 2nd ed., Harlan Davidson, Inc., 2006, p. 86.
4. Cynthia Orozco, *No Mexicans, Women, or Dogs Allowed: The Rise of the Mexican American Civil Rights Movement,* Austin: University of Texas Press, 2009, pp. 50–56.
5. Rudy Acuna, *Occupied America: A History of Chicanos*, Pearson Education, 2014, pp. 202–204.
6. Cynthia Orozco, *No Mexicans, Women, or Dogs Allowed: The Rise of the Mexican American Civil Rights Movement,* Austin: University of Texas Press, 2009, p. 22.
7. Zaragosa Vargas, *Crucible of Struggle: A History of Mexican Americans from the Colonial Period to the Present Era,* Oxford University Press, 2011, pp. 217–220.
8. Neil Foley, *Mexicans in the Making of America*, Belknap Press, 2014, p. 96.
9. Gabriela Gonzalez, *Redeeming La Raza: Transborder Modernity, Race, Respectability, and Right*, New York: Oxford University Press, 2018, pp. 185–186.
10. Lori Flores, *Grounds for Dreaming: Mexican Americans, Mexican Immigrants, and the California Farmworker Movement,* New Haven: Yale University Press, 2016, p. 3.
11. Arnold De Leon and Richard Griswold del Castillo, *North to Aztlan: A History of Mexican Americans in the United States*, 2nd ed., Harlan Davidson, Inc., 2006, pp. 137–138.
12. Ibid., pp. 137–138.
13. Cynthia Orozco, *Agent of Change: Adela Sloss-Vento, Mexican American, Civil Rights Activist, Texas Feminist,* Austin: University of Texas Press, 2020, p. 72.

14. Rudy Acuna, *Occupied America: A History of Chicanos*, Pearson Education, 2014, p. 275.
15. Ibid., pp. 305–306.
16. Ibid., p. 345.
17. Ibid., pp. 345–346.
18. Ibid., p. 345.
19. Ibid., p. 345.
20. Oscar Romero, The Church And El Salvador's Civil War (1983), https://www.youtube.com/watch?v=sQpkonWfbHg.
21. Nicaragua – The Rise and Fall of the Sandinista, 2019, https://www.youtube.com/watch?v=goigdv_4a3o.
22. Cuando Tiemblan Las Montañas – When The Mountains Tremble, 2015, https://www.youtube.com/watch?v=-5Ebib06rX0.
23. Rudy Acuna, *Occupied America: A History of Chicanos*, Pearson Education, 2014, p. 364.
24. 1986: Immigration Reform and Control Act of 1986, https://guides.loc.gov/latinx-civil-rights/irca.
25. Zaragosa Vargas, *Crucible of Struggle: A History of Mexican Americans from the Colonial Period to the Present Era,* Oxford University Press, 2011, p. 354.
26. Rudy Acuna, *Occupied America: A History of Chicanos*, Pearson Education, 2014, pp. 365–366.
27. Zaragosa Vargas, *Crucible of Struggle: A History of Mexican Americans from the Colonial Period to the Present Era,* Oxford University Press, 2011, pp. 384–385.
28. In states where driver's licenses are issued to immigrants, they are adorned with distinction marks, differentiating them from others and indicating that the card holders are zimmigrants.

PART II: *THE TRUTH* IN OUR STORIES

29. National Academies of Sciences, Engineering, and Medicine, *The Economic and Fiscal Consequences of Immigration* (Washington, DC: National Academies Press, 2017), https://doi.org/10.17226/23550.
30. "U.S. Immigration Statistics: Immigrants and the Economy in the United States of America," New American Economy, 2021, https://www.newamericaneconomy.org/locations/national.
31. Pierre Azoulay et al., "Immigration and Entrepreneurship in the United States" (Working Paper 27778, National Bureau of Economic Research, September 2020), http://www.nber.org/papers/w27778.
32. Jessica Love, "Immigrants to the U.S. Create More Jobs than They Take," Kellogg Insight (Kellogg School of Management at Northwestern University, October 5, 2020), https://insight.kellogg.northwestern.edu/article/immigrants-to-the-u-s-create-more-jobs-than-they-take.
33. Donald Kerwin et al., "US Foreign-Born Essential Workers by Status and State, and the Global Pandemic," Center for Migration Studies, May 2020, https://cmsny.org/publications/us-essential-workers.
34. Center for Disease Control and Prevention, "Heat-Related Deaths Among Crop Workers—United States, 1992–2006," *MMWR*, 57, no. 24 (June 20, 2008): 649–653, https://www.cdc.gov/mmwr/preview/mmwrhtml/mm5724a1.htm.

35. "Trump Ends DACA Program, No New Applications Accepted," https://www.nbcnews.com/politics/immigration/trump-dreamers-daca-immigration-announcement-n798686.
36. "Supreme Court Blocks Trump from Ending DACA," https://www.cnn.com/2020/06/18/politics/daca-immigration-supreme-court/index.html.
37. "Top 5 things you need to know about the Texas case on DACA," https://unitedwedream.org/2021/07/top-5-things-you-need-to-know-about-the-texas-case-on-daca/?gclid=Cj0KCQjw_fiLBhDOARIsAF4khR0DD0gIlcI9Tz31eA48ujD5Pw_DxmKYqwUadUFzOgE_FkBU0RLQSDUaAhi1EALw_wcB.
38. "Advocates Fear Mass Suicide at ICE Facility in Southern NM." October 18, 2019, *8 Las Vegas Now*, http://northlasvegas.8newsnow.com/news/1370031-advocates-fear-mass-suicide-ice-facility-southern-nm.
39. "New Tracker Finds 177 Fatal Encounters with Customs and Border Protection (CBP) Since 2010," https://www.aclutx.org/en/press-releases/new-tracker-finds-177-fatal-encounters-customs-and-border-protection-cbp-2010.
40. FY 2016 ICE Immigration Removals." U.S. Immigration and Customs Enforcement, https://www.ice.gov/remove/removal-statistics/2016.
41. "Human Rights First Denounces New Fees for Asylum in the United States," https://www.humanrightsfirst.org/press-release/human-rights-first-denounces-new-fees-asylum-united-states.
42. "The Migrant Protection Protocols," American Immigration Council, https://www.americanimmigrationcouncil.org/research/migrant-protection-protocols.
43. "Police: El Paso shooting suspect said he targeted Mexicans," *AP News*, https://apnews.com/article/shootings-el-paso-texas-mass-shooting-us-news-ap-top-news-immigration-456c0154218a4d378e2fb36cd40b709d.
44. "The Biden Administration Is Fighting In Court To Keep A Trump-Era Immigration Policy," *Houston Public Media*, https://www.npr.org/2021/09/20/1038918197/the-biden-administration-is-fighting-in-court-to-keep-a-trump-era-immigration-po.
45. "U.S. Must Provide Mental Health Services to Families Separated at Border," https://www.nytimes.com/2019/11/06/us/migrants-mental-health-court.html.
46. "Judge Blocks Public Charge Restrictions Due to Pandemic," https://www.cwla.org/judge-blocks-public-charge-restrictions-due-to-pandemic/.

SELECTED BIBLIOGRAPHY

Acuna, Rodolfo F. *Occupied America: A History of Chicanos.* 8th ed. Pearson Education, 2014.

Akers Chacon, Justin, and Mike Davis. *No One Is Illegal: Fighting Racism and State Violence on the U.S.-Mexico Border.* 2nd ed. Haymarket Books, 2018.

Boehm, Deborah A., and Susan J. Terrio. *Illegal Encounter: The Effect of Detention and Deportation on Young People.* New York University Press, 2019.

De Leon, Arnold, and Richard Griswold del Castillo. *North to Aztlan: A History of Mexican Americans in the United States.* 2nd ed. Harlan Davidson, Inc., 2006.

Fernandez, Raul E., and Gilbert Gonzalez. *A Century of Chicano History: Empire, Nations and Migration.* Routledge, 2003.

Foley, Neil. *Mexicans in the Making of America.* Cambridge, MA: Belknap Press, 2014.

Gómez, Laura E. *Manifest Destinies: The Making of the Mexican American Race.* 2nd ed. New York University Press, 2018.

Gonzalez, Gabriela. *Redeeming La Raza: Transborder Modernity, Race, Respectability, and Right.* New York: Oxford University Press, 2018.

Groody, Daniel G., and Gioacchino Campese. *A Promised Land, A Perilous Journey: Theological Perspectives on Migration.* University of Notre Dame Press, 2008.

Gutiérrez, David G. *Between Two Worlds: Mexican Immigrants in the United States.* Rowman & Littlefield, 1996.

Hagan, Jacqueline Maria. *Migration Miracle: Faith, Hope, and Meaning on the Undocumented Journey.* Harvard University Press, 2012.

Kang, S. Deborah. The INS on the Line: *Making Immigration Law on the U.S.-Mexico Border, 1917–1954.* Oxford University Press, 2016.

Levario, Miguel Antonio. *Militarizing the Border: When Mexicans Became the Enemy.* Texas A&M University Press, 2012.

Martinez, Oscar J. *U.S.-Mexico Borderlands: Historical and Contemporary Perspectives.* Rowman & Littlefield, 1996.

Mulligan Sepulveda, J. J. *No Human Is Illegal: An Attorney on the Front Lines of the Immigration War.* New York: Melville House, 2019.

Ngai, Mae M., and Jon Gjerde. *Major Problems in American Immigration History: Documents and Essays.* 2nd ed. Wadsworth Cengage Learning, 2011.

Orozco, Cynthia. *Agent of Change: Adela Sloss-Vento, Mexican American, Civil Rights Activist, Texas Feminist.* Austin: University of Texas Press, 2020.

Orozco, Cynthia. *No Mexicans, Women, or Dogs Allowed: The Rise of the Mexican American Civil Rights Movement.* Austin: University of Texas Press, 2009.

Schwab, William A. *Dreams Derailed: Undocumented Youths in the Trump Era.* University of Arkansas Press, 2018.

Spener, David. *Clandestine Crossings: Migrants and Coyotes on the Texas–Mexico Border.* Cornell University Press, 2009.

Vargas, Zaragosa. *Crucible of Struggle: A History of Mexican Americans from the Colonial Period to the Present Era.* Oxford University Press, 2011.

Ventura Miller, Holly, and Anthony Peguero. *Routledge Handbook on Immigration and Crime.* 1st ed. Routledge, 2018.

Zimmer, William K., and Judith A. Zimmer-Baker. *Approaching the Bench from Inside the Immigration Court.* 4th ed. Manchester Center, VT: Canoe Tree Press, 2021.

CPSIA information can be obtained
at www.ICGtesting.com
Printed in the USA
LVHW061445120622
721079LV00005B/209